ZANZIBAR TRAVEL GUIDE 2025

Your Complete Handbook to Explore Beaches, Culture, and Top Attractions

Christy T Davis

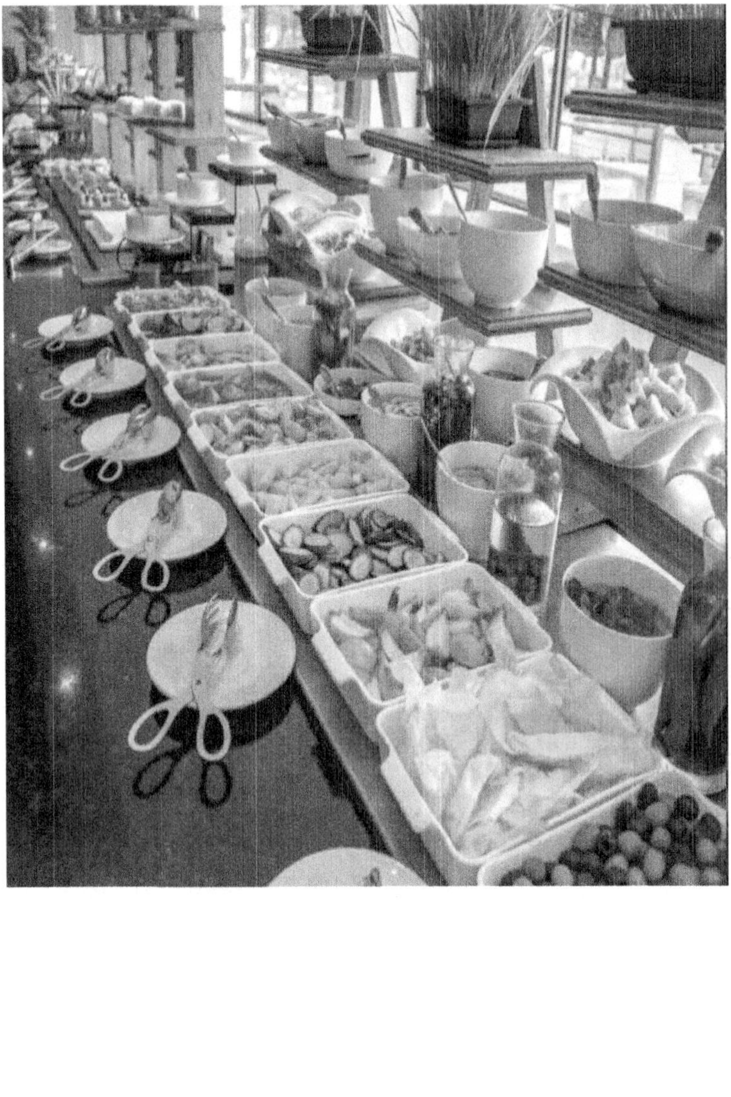

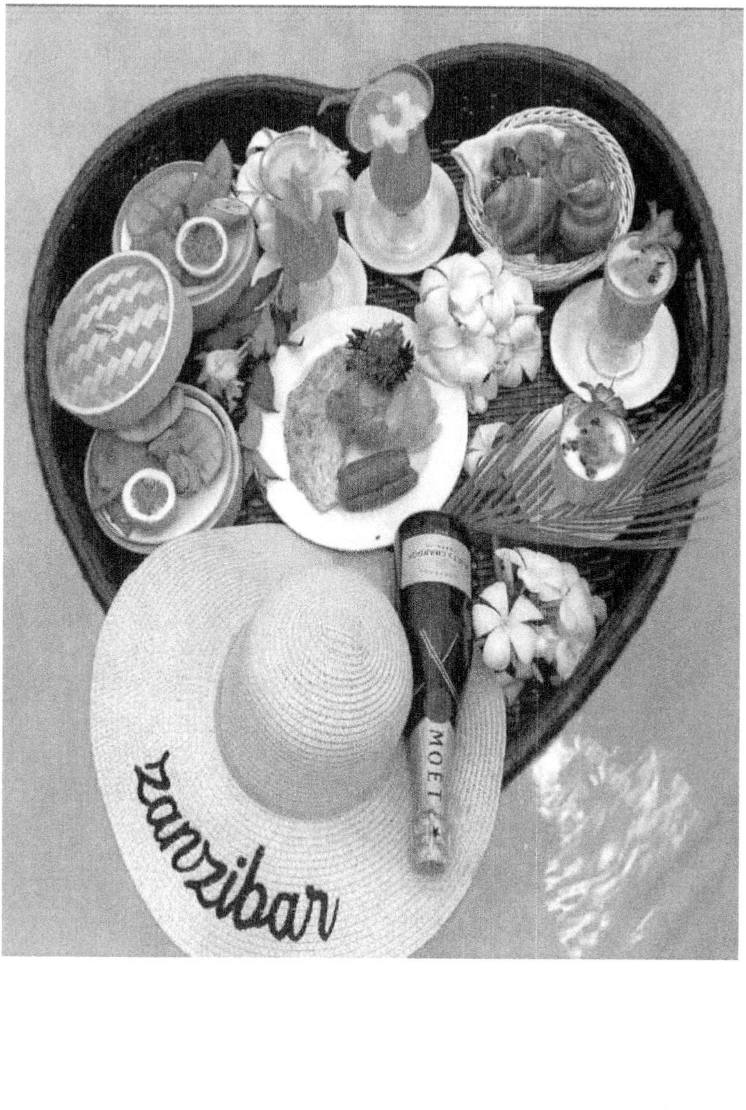
zanzibar
MOET

Copyright © [2024] by [Christy T. Davis].

All rights reserved. No part of this publication may be reproduced, distributed, or transmitted in any form or by any means, including photocopying, recording, or other electronic or mechanical methods, without the prior written permission of the publisher, except in the case of brief quotations embodied in critical reviews and certain other noncommercial uses permitted by copyright law.

Table of contents

Chapter 1: Welcome to Zanzibar
- 1.1. Overview of Zanzibar as a Travel Destination
- 1.2. A Brief History and Cultural Background
- 1.3. Key Reasons to Visit Zanzibar
- 1.4. Best Time to Visit: Weather, Seasons, and Festivals

Chapter 2: Planning Your Trip to Zanzibar
- 2.1. Travel Requirements: Visas and Passports
- 2.2. Choosing Accommodation: Resorts, Hotels, and Guesthouses
- 2.3. Budgeting Your Trip: Costs, Currency, and Tipping
- 2.4. Essential Packing Guide: What to Bring for Your Zanzibar Adventure

Chapter 3: Navigating Stone Town
- 3.1. A Historical Overview of Stone Town
- 3.2. Key Landmarks: The Old Fort, House of Wonders, and Hamamni Baths
- 3.3. Discovering the Sultan's Palace and Slave Market
- 3.4. Wandering the Labyrinth Streets: Culture, Art, and Architecture
- 3.5. Shopping in Stone Town: Markets, Souvenirs, and Local Crafts.
- 3.6. Local Cuisine and Coffee Houses: Where to Eat in Stone Town
- 3.7. Guided Walking Tours: Hidden Gems and

Cultural Insights

Chapter 4: Zanzibar's Top Beaches and Coastal Life

4.1. The Northern Paradise: Nungwi and Kendwa

4.2. Paje and Jambiani: Zanzibar's Kite Surfing and Water Sports Hub

4.3. Exploring the Pristine Sands of Matemwe

4.4. Kizimkazi: Dolphin Spotting and Fishing Villages

4.5. Michamvi Peninsula: Quiet Retreats and Beach Getaways

4.6. Best Beachfront Restaurants and Bars

Chapter 5: Outdoor Adventures and Activities.

5.1. Scuba Diving and Snorkeling: Top Spots and Marine Life

5.2. Kite Surfing: Paje's Famous Winds and Lessons

5.3. Sailing and Deep-Sea Fishing in Zanzibar's Waters

5.4. Safari Blue Tour: Island Hopping and Sandbank Adventures

5.5. Walking and Cycling Trails in Zanzibar

5.6. Birdwatching and Exploring Zanzibar's Wildlife

Chapter 6: Zanzibar's Nature and Wildlife

6.1. Jozani Forest: Exploring the Red Colobus Monkeys

6.2. Mangroves and Wetlands: A Diverse Ecosystem

6.3. Chumbe Island: Coral Reefs and Conservation Projects

6.4. Marine Reserves and Protected Areas in Zanzibar

Chapter 7: Culture and Traditions in Zanzibar

7.1. The Influence of Swahili Culture on Zanzibar's Identity

7.2. Traditional Arts and Crafts: Wood Carving, Tinga Tinga, and Fabrics

7.3. Local Etiquette and Social Customs: Do's and Don'ts for Tourists

Chapter 8: Zanzibar's Food and Culinary Experiences

8.1. Traditional Dishes: Ugali, Pilau, and Zanzibar Pizza

8.2. Seafood Specialties: Fresh Fish, Octopus, and Lobster

8.3. Spice Tour Cuisine: Cooking Classes and Local Delicacies

8.4. Dining Out: Zanzibar's Best Restaurants, Cafés, and Street Food

Chapter 9: Practical Tips for a Stress-Free Visit

9.1. Safety and Health in Zanzibar: Clinics, Hospitals, and Insurance

9.2. Getting Around: Taxis, Daladalas, and Car Rentals

9.3. Internet, SIM Cards, and Staying Connected

9.4. Money Matters: ATMs, Credit Cards, and Local Banks

Chapter 10: Zanzibar's Laws, Customs, and Visitor Etiquette
    10.1. Important Legal Information: Drugs, Alcohol, and Public Behavior
    10.2. Environmental Responsibility: Protecting Zanzibar's Ecosystem
    10.4. Responsible Tourism: Giving Back to the Local Community
Chapter 11. A 5 Days Zanzibar Itinerary
Conclusion

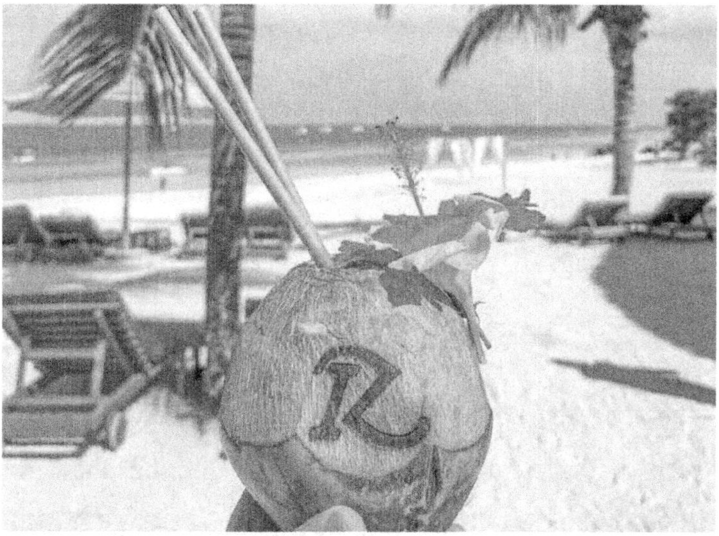

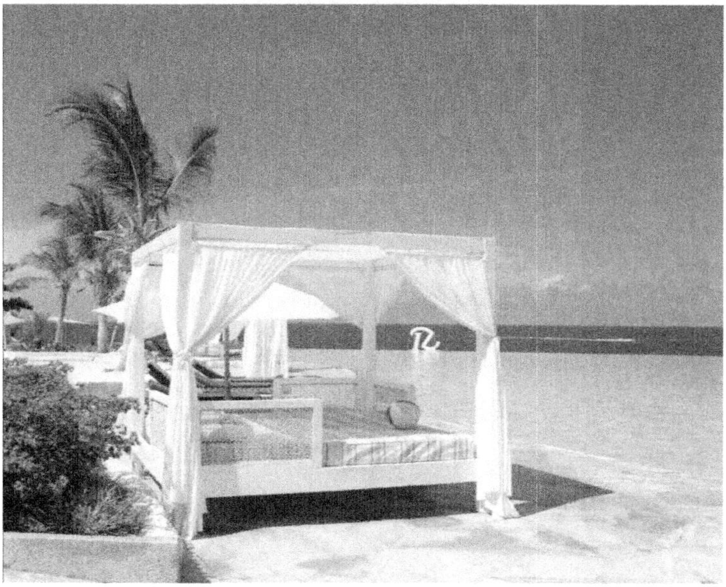

Chapter 1: Welcome to Zanzibar

1.1. Overview of Zanzibar as a Travel Destination

Zanzibar, the Spice Island of the Indian Ocean, beckons with its ancient Stone Town, pristine beaches, and vibrant culture. This semi-autonomous island off the coast of Tanzania has a rich history dating back to the 1st century AD, with a unique blend of African, Arab, and European influences. Wander through the narrow alleys of Stone Town, a UNESCO World Heritage Site, where every corner tells a story. Marvel at the intricate wooden doors, visit the House of Wonders, and immerse yourself in the bustling markets. The town's architecture and layout reflect centuries of cultural exchange, making it a living museum of history.

Zanzibar's beaches are nothing short of spectacular. From the powdery sands of Nungwi and Kendwa in the north to the serene shores of Paje and Jambiani in the east, there's a beach for every type of traveler. The crystal-clear waters are perfect for snorkeling and diving, offering a glimpse into the vibrant marine life and coral reefs. For the adventurous, kite surfing in Paje is a must-try experience.

Zanzibar's culture is as diverse as its history. Engage with the local Swahili culture through traditional music, dance, and cuisine. Don't miss a spice tour to learn why Zanzibar is known as the Spice Island. Visit local farms to see, smell, and taste a variety of spices, from cloves to cinnamon, and understand their significance in Zanzibari cuisine. The island's culinary scene is equally diverse, reflecting its multicultural heritage. Savor traditional Swahili dishes, fresh seafood, and a variety of international cuisines.

With its warm hospitality, rich history, and stunning natural beauty, Zanzibar is a must-visit destination for any traveler. So why wait? Come and discover the magic of Zanzibar for yourself.

1.2. A Brief History and Cultural Background

Zanzibar, an archipelago off the coast of Tanzania, is a place where history and culture intertwine beautifully. This semi-autonomous region has a rich past that dates back over 20,000 years, with its earliest inhabitants being African hunter-gatherers. Over the centuries, Zanzibar became a melting pot of cultures due to its strategic location on ancient trade routes.

The islands first gained prominence as a trading hub for spices, ivory, and slaves. By the 8th century, Arab and Persian traders had established settlements, bringing Islam and building the first mosques in the region. This period marked the beginning of Zanzibar's transformation into a cultural crossroads.

Early Trade and Settlement

Zanzibar, an island paradise, has a history that dates back to the 1st Century AD. Traders from Arabia, Persia, and India began arriving by navigating the monsoon winds. These early traders established wealthy port cities along the coast, with a significant harbor at what is now Zanzibar City. Although the islands themselves lacked substantial resources, Zanzibar's strategic location made it an ideal hub for trade and exploration along the East African coast. It also served as a crucial stopover for traders heading to Asia, the Middle East, and the African interior. Over time, some Persian traders settled permanently in Stone Town, leaving a lasting influence on the island's architecture, cuisine, and culture. Notably, the village of Kizimkazi on Zanzibar's southern coast is home to one of the earliest mosques in the southern hemisphere, built by Yemeni traders in 1107.

Portuguese Influence

The arrival of Portuguese explorer Vasco da Gama in 1499 marked the beginning of European influence in Zanzibar. The islands became part of the Portuguese

Empire, although the Portuguese ruled from a distance, relying on mutual assistance with local leaders. The Portuguese established a trading factory and Christian mission in modern-day Zanzibar City, and some Portuguese settlers became farmers on the islands. The relationship between the Portuguese and the Zanzibari leaders was generally cooperative, with the Zanzibaris assisting the Portuguese in various military endeavors.

Omani Rule and Economic Boom

In 1698, the Arab rulers of Oman captured Mombasa from the Portuguese, bringing Zanzibar under Omani control. This period saw a significant increase in trade, particularly in ivory and slaves, as well as the export of cloves. Stone Town became one of the wealthiest and largest cities in East Africa. Traders from Arabia, Persia, and India continued to arrive, bringing goods such as iron, cloth, sugar, and dates, and leaving with tortoiseshell, cloves, coconuts, rice, ivory, and slaves. The wealth generated from these trades transformed Zanzibar into a bustling economic center.

British Influence and Independence

Zanzibar's strategic importance continued into the 19th and 20th centuries. The British established a protectorate over the islands in the late 19th century, which lasted until Zanzibar gained independence in 1963. The following year, Zanzibar merged with Tanganyika to form the United Republic of Tanzania. Despite these political changes, Zanzibar has retained a degree of autonomy and continues to be a unique blend of African, Arab, and European influences.

Modern Zanzibar

Today, Zanzibar remains a semi-autonomous region of Tanzania, known for its rich cultural heritage and historical significance. The island's history is reflected in its diverse architecture, vibrant markets, and the enduring traditions of its people. Visitors to Zanzibar can explore the remnants of its storied past, from the ancient mosques and palaces to the bustling streets of Stone Town, a UNESCO World Heritage site.

Zanzibar's history is a testament to its role as a crossroads of cultures and a hub of trade and exploration. Its unique blend of influences makes it a fascinating destination for travelers interested in history, culture, and the enduring legacy of this island paradise.

1.3. Key Reasons to Visit Zanzibar

Zanzibar's reputation as an island paradise is not an exaggeration; it is an archipelago in the Indian Ocean off the coast of Tanzania, consisting of two large islands—Ungoja (commonly referred to as Zanzibar) and Pemba—along with several smaller islands, featuring an entire eastern coast with miles of pristine sandy beaches, amazing coral reefs, a relaxed atmosphere, and seafood dishes that will make your holiday memorable, especially if you are a beach or sun lover with a passion for snorkeling:

1. Stunning Beaches

Zanzibar boasts some of the most beautiful beaches in the world, with powdery white sand and crystal-clear turquoise waters. Whether you're looking to relax or engage in water sports, the beaches of Nungwi, Kendwa, and Paje offer something for everyone.

2. Rich Cultural Heritage

Stone Town, the cultural heart of Zanzibar, is a UNESCO World Heritage site. Its narrow alleys, bustling bazaars, and historic buildings reflect a rich blend of Arab, Persian, Indian, and European influences. Exploring Stone Town is like stepping back in time.

3. World-Class Diving and Snorkeling

The coral reefs surrounding Zanzibar are teeming with marine life, making it a top destination for diving and snorkeling. Sites like Mnemba Atoll offer the chance to see colorful fish, sea turtles, and even dolphins.

4. Spice Tours

Known as the "Spice Island," Zanzibar is famous for its spice plantations. A spice tour offers a fascinating insight into the island's history and economy, as well as the chance to see, smell, and taste a variety of spices, including cloves, nutmeg, and cinnamon.

5. Unique Wildlife

Zanzibar is home to the Jozani Forest, where you can see the rare red colobus monkeys, unique to the island. The forest also offers a chance to explore mangrove swamps and spot other wildlife.

6. Delicious Cuisine

Zanzibari cuisine is a delightful fusion of African, Arab, Indian, and European flavors. From fresh seafood to aromatic spices, the local dishes are a treat for the taste buds. Don't miss trying dishes like biryani, pilau, and the famous Zanzibar pizza.

7. Vibrant Markets

The markets in Zanzibar, especially in Stone Town, are vibrant and colorful. They offer a wide range of goods, from fresh produce and spices to handmade crafts and souvenirs. The Darajani Market is a must-visit for an authentic local experience.

8. Historical Sites

Zanzibar has a rich history, and there are many historical sites to explore. The House of Wonders, the Old Fort, and the Sultan's Palace are just a few of the landmarks that tell the story of the island's past.

9. Friendly Locals

The people of Zanzibar are known for their warmth and hospitality. Interacting with the locals can provide a deeper understanding of the island's culture and traditions.

10. Sustainable Tourism

Zanzibar is committed to sustainable tourism practices. Many eco-friendly lodges and tours are available, ensuring that your visit supports the local community and preserves the natural environment.

These reasons make Zanzibar a captivating destination for travelers seeking a mix of relaxation, adventure, and cultural enrichment. Whether you're lounging on the beach, exploring historical sites, or diving into the vibrant underwater world, Zanzibar promises an unforgettable experience.

1.4. Best Time to Visit: Weather, Seasons, and Festivals

Zanzibar, with its stunning beaches, rich cultural heritage, and vibrant festivals, is a year-round destination. However, understanding the weather patterns and seasonal highlights can help you plan the perfect trip.

Weather and Seasons

1. Dry Season (June to October)

The best time to visit Zanzibar is during the dry season, from June to October. This period offers warm, sunny days with minimal rainfall, making it ideal for beach activities, diving, and exploring the island. Daytime temperatures range from 25°C to 30°C (77°F to 86°F), and the sea is perfect for swimming.

2. Short Dry Season (January to February)

Another great time to visit is during the short dry season in January and February. The weather is hot and dry, with temperatures slightly higher than the main dry season. This period is less crowded than the peak summer months, offering a more relaxed atmosphere.

3. Long Rainy Season (March to May)

The long rainy season, known as "Masika," occurs from March to May. During this time, Zanzibar experiences heavy tropical downpours, high humidity, and fewer tourists. While some businesses may close, this season offers a unique, lush landscape and lower prices for accommodation.

4. Short Rainy Season (November to December)

The short rainy season, or "Vuli," happens in November and December. These rains are lighter and less predictable than the long rains, often occurring in brief morning showers. This period can still be a good time to visit if you prefer fewer crowds and don't mind occasional rain.

Daytime temperatures in Zanzibar are consistently pleasant throughout the year. During the hot season, maximum temperatures rarely exceed the mid-30s Celsius (around 90°F), while the rainy seasons are about 3-4 degrees cooler. Nighttime temperatures generally do not drop below a mild 21°C (70°F) at any time of the year. The sea remains warm enough for swimming year-round, ranging from 25°C (77°F) in August to 29°C (84°F) from December to April.

Festivals and Events

1. Sauti za Busara (February)

One of East Africa's most celebrated music festivals, Sauti za Busara, takes place in Stone Town every February. The festival features a diverse lineup of African music, dance, and cultural performances, attracting artists and visitors from around the world.

2. Zanzibar International Film Festival (July)

Held annually in July, the Zanzibar International Film Festival (ZIFF) is the largest cultural event in East Africa. It showcases films, documentaries, and shorts from African and international filmmakers, along with workshops, exhibitions, and musical performances.

3. Mwaka Kogwa (July/August)

Mwaka Kogwa is a traditional Shirazi New Year celebration held in the village of Makunduchi. This four-day festival, usually in July or August, includes rituals, singing, dancing, and mock fights, symbolizing the cleansing of past grievances and the welcoming of a prosperous new year.

4. Eid al-Fitr and Eid al-Adha

As a predominantly Muslim region, Zanzibar celebrates Eid al-Fitr and Eid al-Adha with great enthusiasm. These festivals mark the end of Ramadan and the annual pilgrimage to Mecca, respectively. Visitors can experience local customs, feasts, and community gatherings during these times.

5. Zanzibar Food Festival (October): A celebration of local cuisine, this festival features food stalls, cooking demonstrations, and cultural performances, making it a must-visit for food lovers.

Zanzibar's sun-kissed beaches, vibrant cultural festivals, and captivating history make it a unique and unforgettable travel destination, no matter what draws you to this enchanting spice island.

Chapter 2: Planning Your Trip to Zanzibar

2.1. Travel Requirements: Visas and Passports

When planning an international trip, understanding the visa and passport requirements for your destination is crucial.

Passports

1. Validity

Ensure your passport is valid for at least six months beyond your planned departure date. Many countries enforce this rule to avoid issues with travelers overstaying their visas.

2. Blank Pages

Check that your passport has enough blank pages for entry and exit stamps. Some countries require at least two blank pages.

3. Renewal

If your passport is nearing expiration, renew it well in advance of your trip. Processing times can vary, so it's best to apply early to avoid any last-minute issues.

Visas

1. Visa Requirements

Visa requirements vary by country and depend on your nationality. Some countries allow visa-free entry for short stays, while others require a visa obtained in advance or upon arrival. It's essential to check the specific requirements for your destination.

2. Types of Visas

- Tourist Visa: For leisure travel and short stays.

- Business Visa: For attending meetings, conferences, or conducting business.
- Student Visa: For studying abroad.
- Work Visa: For employment in a foreign country.
- Transit Visa: For passing through a country en route to another destination.

3. Application Process

The visa application process typically involves filling out an application form, providing a valid passport, passport-sized photos, and supporting documents such as proof of accommodation, travel itinerary, and financial means. Some countries may also require an interview or biometric data.

4. Visa on Arrival and e-Visas

Many countries offer visas on arrival or electronic visas (e-Visas) for added convenience. These options allow travelers to apply online and receive their visa electronically, reducing the need for a visit to an embassy or consulate.

Additional Considerations

1. Travel Insurance

While not always mandatory, travel insurance is highly recommended. It can cover medical emergencies, trip cancellations, and other unforeseen events.

2. Health Requirements

Some countries require proof of vaccinations or health certificates, especially for diseases like yellow fever. Check the health requirements for your destination and ensure you have the necessary documentation.

3. Entry and Exit Fees

Be aware of any entry or exit fees that may apply. These fees are sometimes included in your airline ticket, but in some cases, they must be paid separately upon arrival or departure.

4. Registration with Embassies

For added safety, consider registering with your home country's embassy or consulate in your destination country. This can provide assistance in case of emergencies and keep you informed about safety updates.

By understanding and preparing for the visa and passport requirements of your destination, you can ensure a smooth and hassle-free travel experience. Always check the latest information from official sources or your destination's embassy to stay updated on any changes in travel regulations.

2.2. Choosing Accommodation: Resorts, Hotels, and Guesthouses

Zanzibar offers a range of accommodation options to suit different preferences and budgets, from luxurious retreats and comfortable hotels to charming guesthouses and everything in between.

Resorts

1. The Residence Zanzibar

Located on the southwestern coast, The Residence Zanzibar is a luxurious resort with private villas, each with its own plunge pool. The resort is set in lush tropical gardens along a pristine beach. Guests can indulge in world-class spa treatments, enjoy fine dining with a focus on local and international flavors, and take part in water sports like snorkeling and kayaking.

2. Baraza Resort and Spa

Baraza is an all-inclusive luxury resort located on the famous Bwejuu beach. It offers a mix of Swahili and Arabic design, with spacious villas adorned in handcrafted furniture and fabrics. The resort features a tranquil spa, private pools, and a range of activities like kite surfing, reef walking, and yoga.

3. Zuri Zanzibar

Located in Kendwa, Zuri Zanzibar is an eco-conscious resort blending luxury with sustainability. It boasts stunning bungalows, suites, and beachfront villas. The resort is known for its exceptional culinary offerings, lush spice gardens, and its focus on wellness, offering yoga sessions, massages, and meditation.

4. Mnemba Island Lodge

For a truly exclusive experience, Mnemba Island Lodge is a private island paradise surrounded by coral reefs. With only 12 beachside bandas, the lodge offers unparalleled seclusion. Guests can enjoy scuba diving, deep-sea fishing, and whale watching. The lodge also practices eco-friendly tourism, supporting local marine conservation efforts.

5. Melia Zanzibar

Situated on a large estate with tropical gardens and a private white sandy beach, Melia Zanzibar offers a wide variety of rooms, from garden rooms to beachfront villas. The resort features several restaurants and bars, an infinity pool, and a world-class spa. Activities include paddleboarding, tennis, and cultural tours to Stone Town and spice farms.

Hotels

1. Park Hyatt Zanzibar

Located in the heart of Stone Town, Park Hyatt Zanzibar combines modern luxury with traditional Zanzibari architecture. Its prime location offers views of the ocean and easy access to key historical sites. The hotel features a rooftop infinity pool, a spa, and gourmet dining, making it ideal for travelers who want a luxurious stay while exploring the cultural heart of Zanzibar.

2. Zanzibar Serena Hotel

Another gem in Stone Town, Zanzibar Serena Hotel offers an elegant blend of Swahili and Arabic influences. It's renowned for its attention to detail, from intricately carved woodwork to lavishly decorated rooms. Guests can relax by the pool, dine at the oceanfront restaurant, or explore the vibrant surroundings, including the House of Wonders and the Old Fort.

3. DoubleTree by Hilton Hotel Zanzibar - Stone Town
A blend of modern amenities and traditional charm, this centrally located hotel offers comfortable rooms with a Zanzibari twist. It's within walking distance of key attractions, making it convenient for sightseeing. The rooftop restaurant serves local and international cuisine, offering stunning views of the town and the sea.

4. Tembo House Hotel
Located along the beachfront in Stone Town, Tembo House is a heritage hotel with authentic Zanzibari decor. The rooms feature wooden beds and hand-carved furniture, offering a unique cultural experience. It has a swimming pool and easy access to the beach, providing a peaceful retreat after exploring the busy streets of Stone Town.

5. Zanzibar Queen Hotel
Set in the peaceful area of Matemwe, Zanzibar Queen Hotel is a great mid-range option for those seeking comfort near some of the island's best diving and snorkeling spots. The hotel offers beautifully designed

rooms, a serene pool, and a restaurant serving fresh seafood and local delicacies.

Guesthouses

1. Emerson on Hurumzi

Emerson on Hurumzi is a boutique guesthouse in the heart of Stone Town, offering an authentic Zanzibari experience. The rooms are richly decorated in Swahili style, featuring ornate beds and traditional fabrics. The rooftop tea house restaurant offers panoramic views of the city and the ocean, and the sunset dinners are a highlight.

2. Kholle House

This charming guesthouse is a lovingly restored 19th-century palace built by Princess Kholle. It offers individually decorated rooms blending African, French, and Arabian influences. Guests can enjoy the serene garden, rooftop terrace with sea views, and a small swimming pool. The central location is perfect for exploring Stone Town.

3. Jambiani Villas

Located in the village of Jambiani on Zanzibar's east coast, Jambiani Villas offers a laid-back, homely atmosphere. The beachfront guesthouse features spacious self-catering villas, making it ideal for families or groups. The calm, turquoise waters and nearby coral reef make it perfect for snorkeling and kayaking.

4. Mbuyuni Beach Village

This affordable guesthouse in Jambiani provides simple but comfortable bungalows set in a tropical garden. The relaxed atmosphere, combined with its beachfront location, makes it a favorite among backpackers and budget travelers. There's an onsite restaurant offering local and international dishes, and plenty of hammocks for lounging.

5. Stone Town Café and Bed & Breakfast

A small but charming guesthouse in the heart of Stone Town, Stone Town Café offers a personal touch with its friendly staff and homey vibe. The rooms are clean and comfortable, and breakfast is served in the café downstairs, which is also popular with locals. It's an ideal base for budget-conscious travelers exploring the city's winding streets.

Choosing the right accommodation in Zanzibar depends on the type of experience you want. Whether you're looking for the ultimate luxury at a secluded resort, the convenience of a hotel in Stone Town, or the cozy charm of a guesthouse, these hand-picked recommendations ensure a memorable stay in this island paradise.

2.3. Budgeting Your Trip: Costs, Currency, and Tipping

When planning your trip to Zanzibar, it's important to consider various factors that will affect your overall budget, from accommodation and activities to currency exchange and tipping, and to ensure you make the most of your travel experience without overspending by carefully managing costs, understanding currency, and navigating tipping practices.

Costs

Accommodation:

- Budget: If you're traveling on a budget, guesthouses and budget hotels offer rooms ranging from $30 to $70 per night. These accommodations are often basic but comfortable, particularly in areas like Stone Town or Jambiani.

- Mid-range: Mid-range hotels and boutique guesthouses can range from $70 to $150 per night. These typically offer more amenities, such as pools, restaurants, and beachfront locations.

- Luxury: High-end resorts and luxury hotels range from $200 to $600 or more per night. These properties often include private villas, spa services, fine dining, and access to exclusive beaches and activities.

Food & Drink:

- Street Food: For a taste of local cuisine, street food can cost as little as $3 to $10 per meal. Favorites like zanzibar pizza, samosas, and grilled seafood are affordable and delicious.

- Local Restaurants: Dining at local restaurants can range from $10 to $20 per person. These offer a mix of Swahili, Indian, and international dishes, with fresh seafood often being a highlight.
- Upscale Dining: For fine dining experiences, especially at resort restaurants, expect to pay around $30 to $50 per person, with higher-end options including wine and cocktails.

Activities & Excursions:
- Cultural and Historical Tours: Visiting historical sites like Stone Town's Slave Market or a spice plantation tour can cost $20 to $50 per person. Guided tours are available and often enhance the experience.
- Water Sports & Outdoor Activities: Snorkeling trips, dhow cruises, and kite surfing can cost between $30 and $100, depending on the length of the activity and the level of service.
- Safari Blue Experience: A full-day tour of Zanzibar's marine life, including snorkeling, island hopping, and a seafood feast, ranges from $70 to $100 per person.

Currency

The local currency is the Tanzanian Shilling (TZS). However, the U.S. Dollar (USD) is widely accepted in most tourist areas, especially for larger transactions like hotel stays, tours, and transport. That said, it's advisable to carry some Tanzanian Shillings for smaller purchases like food, drinks, and souvenirs, especially when dealing with local vendors.

- Exchange Rates: Currency exchange services are available at airports, banks, and major hotels, but it's often better to use ATMs for cash withdrawals, as they tend to offer better exchange rates. Be aware of withdrawal fees, which may apply.
- Credit Cards: Major hotels, restaurants, and tour companies accept credit cards, but smaller businesses and local markets may not. It's a good idea to carry cash for smaller transactions.
- Currency Tip: Always check if prices are listed in TZS or USD to avoid confusion when paying for goods or services.

Tipping

Tipping is not mandatory in Zanzibar, but it is appreciated for good service, particularly in the tourism and hospitality industries.

- Restaurants: If service is not included in the bill, a tip of 10% is standard. For higher-end dining, you may wish to tip more, especially if the service is exceptional.

- Hotels: It is customary to tip hotel staff for services like baggage handling, housekeeping, and room service. A small tip of $1 to $2 per service is appreciated. For longer stays, tipping housekeeping staff a few dollars at the end of your stay is a kind gesture.

- Tour Guides & Drivers: For guided tours, tipping your guide $10 to $20 per day is a common practice, especially if they have provided insightful and engaging service. For drivers or boat captains, a tip of $5 to $10 is appreciated.

- Local Markets: While tipping isn't expected in local markets, rounding up your bill or offering a small amount of change when purchasing items is a nice way to show appreciation.

Budgeting your trip to Zanzibar involves considering the costs of accommodation, food, activities, and transportation, while being mindful of the currency exchange and tipping etiquette.

2.4. Essential Packing Guide: What to Bring for Your Zanzibar Adventure

Packing wisely for Zanzibar ensures a comfortable and enjoyable trip, whether you're planning to relax on the beach, explore historical sites, or embark on water-based activities.

1. Clothing

Lightweight, Breathable Fabrics: Zanzibar's tropical climate can be hot and humid, so packing lightweight and breathable fabrics like cotton or linen is essential. Stick to light colors to stay cool.

- T-shirts and Tank Tops: Pack plenty of lightweight tops for hot days.
- Shorts and Skirts: Comfortable and cool for beach walks or casual sightseeing.
- Swimwear: Bring at least two swimsuits if you plan to spend time at the beach or pool.
- Cover-ups and Sarongs: These are ideal for wearing over swimwear, especially when moving between the beach and public areas.

Modest Clothing for Cultural Sensitivity:

Zanzibar is a predominantly Muslim region, and while beachwear is fine at resorts, modest clothing is recommended in towns and villages.

- Long Skirts or Pants: These are perfect for walking around Stone Town or visiting local markets.
- Lightweight Shawl or Scarf: Use it to cover your shoulders when visiting religious sites or walking through towns.

Footwear:
- Sandals/Flip-Flops: Comfortable for beach and casual wear.
- Walking Shoes: Bring sturdy shoes for exploring Stone Town or hiking.
- Water Shoes: Useful if you plan on snorkeling or swimming near coral reefs.

2. Health and Safety Essentials

Sunscreen: Zanzibar's tropical sun can be intense, so bring high-SPF sunscreen. Reef-safe sunscreen is a great option to protect the marine life if you're swimming or diving.

Insect Repellent: Mosquitoes can be a concern, especially in the evenings or in more rural areas. Choose a repellent containing DEET or a natural alternative.

First-Aid Kit: It's always a good idea to bring a basic first-aid kit with items such as band-aids, antiseptic cream, pain relievers, and motion sickness tablets if you plan on taking boat rides.

Medications: Ensure you have enough prescription medications for the duration of your trip. It's also recommended to take anti-malarial medication, as Zanzibar is a malaria-prone area.

3. Travel Documents and Money

Passport and Visa: Ensure your passport is valid for at least six months beyond your travel dates. Most visitors need a visa to enter Tanzania, which can be obtained online or on arrival.

Vaccination Records: Carry a copy of your yellow fever vaccination certificate, as it is required for travelers arriving from certain countries.

Cash and Cards: Bring U.S. dollars in small denominations for easier transactions, as they are widely accepted. You should also have Tanzanian Shillings for local markets and smaller purchases. Credit cards are accepted at most hotels and larger restaurants, but carrying cash is essential for rural areas and small businesses.

4. Beach and Adventure Gear

Snorkeling Gear (Optional): If you plan to snorkel, you can rent gear, but many prefer to bring their own mask, snorkel, and fins for comfort and quality.

Reef-Safe Flip-Flops: Useful for walking on rocky areas or protecting your feet from sharp coral in the water.

Waterproof Bag: Great for keeping your belongings dry during boat trips or beach activities.

Reusable Water Bottle: Stay hydrated while reducing plastic waste by bringing a durable, reusable water bottle.

5. Tech and Gadgets

Camera or GoPro: Zanzibar is incredibly photogenic, with stunning beaches, marine life, and historical sites. A camera or waterproof GoPro will help you capture the best moments.

Power Bank: Ensure your phone and camera stay charged throughout the day by bringing a portable charger.

Universal Adapter: Zanzibar uses Type G plugs (the same as the UK), so bring a universal adapter if needed.

Waterproof Phone Case: For protecting your phone during water activities or unexpected rain.

6. Miscellaneous Essentials

Guidebook or Maps: Even if you have a smartphone, a guidebook or printed map can be useful for exploring areas with limited cell service.

Reading Material: A good book or Kindle is perfect for relaxing on the beach or at your hotel.

Light Backpack or Daypack: Ideal for day trips, holding essentials like water, sunscreen, and cameras as you explore.

Final Tips

- Pack Light: Zanzibar's laid-back vibe and warm weather mean you won't need a lot of heavy clothing or formal wear. Stick to versatile, lightweight items.
- Stay Organized: Use packing cubes to keep your items organized, making it easy to find essentials during your trip.

By packing the right essentials, you'll be prepared for every part of your Zanzibar adventure, from cultural sightseeing in Stone Town to sun-soaked beach days along the coast.

Chapter 3: Navigating Stone Town

3.1. A Historical Overview of Stone Town

Stone Town, the historic heart of Zanzibar City, is a place where history, culture, and architecture intertwine to tell the story of centuries past. Located on the western coast of Unguja, the main island of the Zanzibar Archipelago, Stone Town is a UNESCO World Heritage site renowned for its unique blend of Arab, Persian, Indian, and European influences.

Early History and Trade

Stone Town's history dates back to the 11th century when it was established as a trading port by the Swahili people. This early settlement thrived due to its strategic location along the Indian Ocean trade routes, facilitating commerce between Africa, the Arabian Peninsula,

Persia, and India. The town's name derives from the grand stone houses built by Arab traders in the 19th century, using coral stone that gives the buildings their distinctive reddish hue.

Portuguese and Omani Influence
In the late 15th century, Portuguese explorer Vasco da Gama arrived in Zanzibar, marking the beginning of European influence. The Portuguese controlled the island for nearly two centuries, establishing it as a key trading post. However, their dominance waned in the late 17th century when the Omani Arabs took control.

Under Omani rule, Stone Town flourished as a major center for the spice trade and the Indian Ocean slave trade. The town's architecture from this period reflects the wealth and cultural diversity brought by traders and settlers from various regions. The Omani sultans built grand palaces, mosques, and fortifications, many of which still stand today.

British Protectorate and Independence

In the late 19th century, Zanzibar became a British protectorate. During this period, Stone Town continued to grow, with the British influencing the island's administration and infrastructure. The abolition of the slave trade in the late 19th century marked a significant shift in the town's economy and social structure.

Zanzibar gained independence from British rule in 1963, and shortly after, in 1964, it merged with Tanganyika to form the United Republic of Tanzania. Despite these political changes, Stone Town retained its cultural and historical significance, becoming a symbol of Zanzibar's rich heritage.

Modern Stone Town

Today, Stone Town is a vibrant cultural hub, attracting visitors from around the world. Its narrow alleys, bustling bazaars, and historic buildings offer a glimpse into the past. Key landmarks include the House of Wonders, the Old Fort, and the Sultan's Palace, each telling a part of the town's storied history.

The town's architecture is characterized by large verandas, intricately carved wooden doors, and coral stone buildings. These features reflect the diverse influences that have shaped Stone Town over the centuries. The town's economy now heavily relies on tourism, with many of its historic sites and cultural festivals drawing international attention.

Stone Town's rich history and cultural heritage make it a must-visit destination for anyone interested in the history of East Africa and the Indian Ocean trade. Its unique blend of influences and well-preserved architecture provide a fascinating window into the past, ensuring that Stone Town remains a living museum of Zanzibar's storied past.

3.2. Key Landmarks: The Old Fort, House of Wonders, and Hamamni Baths

The Old Fort (Ngome Kongwe)

The Old Fort, also known as Ngome Kongwe, is the oldest building in Stone Town and a significant historical landmark. Built by the Omani Arabs in the late 17th century after expelling the Portuguese, the fort served as a defensive structure to protect against invasions. The fort's high, brown walls enclose an inner courtyard that has been transformed into a cultural center. Today, it hosts various events, including the Zanzibar International Film Festival and Sauti za Busara music festival. Visitors can explore the amphitheater, curio shops, and a small museum within the fort.

House of Wonders (Beit-al-Ajaib)

The House of Wonders, or Beit-al-Ajaib, is one of Stone Town's most iconic buildings. Constructed in 1883 by Sultan Barghash bin Said, it was the first building in

Zanzibar to have electricity and an elevator, hence its name. The building's architecture features wide verandas supported by cast-iron columns and high ceilings, reflecting a blend of Swahili and European styles. Although it suffered damage during the Anglo-Zanzibar War, it was later restored and now houses the Museum of History and Culture of Zanzibar and the Swahili Coast. The museum showcases artifacts and exhibits that highlight the rich cultural heritage of Zanzibar.

Hamamni Persian Baths

The Hamamni Persian Baths were built between 1870 and 1888 for Sultan Barghash bin Said and were designed by Shirazi architects. These public baths were a significant social hub in Stone Town, featuring a complex structure with hot and cold baths, toilets, shaving areas, and a restaurant. Although the baths ceased operation in 1920, the building remains a popular tourist attraction. Visitors can explore the various rooms and learn about the historical significance of the baths. The name "Hamamni" means "the place of the baths," and the site offers a glimpse into the daily life and social customs of Zanzibar's past.

These landmarks provide a fascinating insight into the history and culture of Stone Town, making them must-visit sites for anyone exploring Zanzibar.

3.3. Discovering the Sultan's Palace and Slave Market

Sultan's Palace (Beit al-Sahel)

The Sultan's Palace, also known as Beit al-Sahel, is one of the most significant historical buildings in Stone Town, Zanzibar. Located along Mizingani Road on the seafront, it was originally built in the late 19th century to serve as the residence for the Sultan's family. The palace stands on the site of a previous structure that was destroyed during the Anglo-Zanzibar War of 1896.

After the Zanzibar Revolution in 1964, the palace was renamed the People's Palace and used as a government seat. In 1994, it was transformed into a museum dedicated to the history of the Zanzibari royal family. The museum features exhibits on Sultan Sir Khalifa bin Harub and Sayyida Salme (Emily Ruete), a former Zanzibari princess who fled to Germany. Visitors can explore the sultan's family's belongings, including furniture, clothing, and personal items, providing a glimpse into life in Zanzibar during the 19th century.

Old Slave Market

The Old Slave Market in Stone Town is a poignant reminder of Zanzibar's dark history as a major center for the East African slave trade. Located at the site of the former slave market, the Anglican Cathedral Church of Christ now stands as a symbol of emancipation. The market was one of the largest and last open slave markets in the world, operating until it was shut down by the British in 1873.

The site includes a memorial and several preserved chambers were enslaved people were held before being sold. The memorial, unveiled in 1998, features sculptures and plaques that commemorate the suffering endured by the enslaved individuals. Inside the cathedral, a circle of white stones marks the location of the former whipping post, where enslaved people were brutally tested for their endurance. The site serves as a powerful educational resource, highlighting the atrocities of the slave trade and the resilience of those who fought for freedom.

Visiting these landmarks offers a deep and moving insight into Zanzibar's complex history, from the opulence of the Sultan's Palace to the harrowing realities of the slave market. These sites are essential for understanding the cultural and historical fabric of Stone Town.

3.4. Wandering the Labyrinth Streets: Culture, Art, and Architecture

Exploring the labyrinthine streets of Stone Town, Zanzibar, is like stepping into a living museum where every corner reveals a piece of history, culture, and artistic expression. The narrow alleys, bustling markets, and historic buildings create a unique atmosphere that captivates visitors.

Culture

1. Diverse Influences

Stone Town is a melting pot of cultures, reflecting its history as a major trading hub. The influences of Arab, Persian, Indian, and European traders are evident in the town's customs, cuisine, and daily life. This cultural diversity is celebrated through various festivals and events, such as the Sauti za Busara music festival and the Zanzibar International Film Festival.

2. Local Markets

The markets in Stone Town, such as Darajani Market, are vibrant centers of local life. Here, you can experience the hustle and bustle of daily commerce, with stalls selling everything from fresh produce and spices to handmade crafts and textiles. These markets offer a glimpse into the local way of life and are perfect for picking up unique souvenirs.

Art

1. Street Art and Murals

Stone Town's streets are adorned with colorful murals and street art that reflect the island's rich cultural heritage and contemporary issues. These artworks often depict scenes from daily life, historical events, and social messages, adding a vibrant layer to the town's visual landscape.

2. Art Galleries

Several art galleries in Stone Town showcase the work of local and international artists. The Cultural Arts Centre Zanzibar and the Zanzibar Gallery are notable venues where you can explore a variety of artistic styles and mediums, from traditional paintings to modern sculptures.

Architecture

1. Historic Buildings

Stone Town is renowned for its well-preserved historic buildings, many of which date back to the 19th century. The architecture is a blend of Swahili, Arab, Persian, Indian, and European styles, characterized by large verandas, intricately carved wooden doors, and coral stone structures.

2. Iconic Landmarks

- The Old Fort (Ngome Kongwe): Built by the Omani Arabs in the late 17th century, this fort is the oldest building in Stone Town and now serves as a cultural center.

- House of Wonders (Beit-al-Ajaib): Constructed in 1883, this building was the first in Zanzibar to have electricity and an elevator. It now houses the Museum of History and Culture of Zanzibar and the Swahili Coast.

- Hamamni Persian Baths: Built in the late 19th century, these baths were a social hub in Stone Town and are now a popular tourist attraction.

3. Traditional Doors

One of the most distinctive features of Stone Town's architecture is its elaborately carved wooden doors. These doors often feature intricate designs and inscriptions, reflecting the wealth and status of the original owners. They are a testament to the town's rich artistic heritage and craftsmanship.

Wandering through the labyrinthine streets of Stone Town offers a unique opportunity to immerse yourself in the rich tapestry of Zanzibar's culture, art, and architecture. Each turn reveals a new story, making it a truly unforgettable experience.

3.5. Shopping in Stone Town: Markets, Souvenirs, and Local Crafts.

Stone Town, the historical heart of Zanzibar, is a bustling maze of narrow streets filled with vibrant markets, unique souvenirs, and local crafts that reflect the island's rich cultural heritage. Whether you're looking for spices, textiles, or hand-carved artwork, Stone Town offers a treasure trove of items to bring home.

1. Markets: A Bustling Hub of Activity

Shopping in Stone Town often begins at its lively markets, where locals and visitors alike gather to trade, bargain, and explore. These markets are filled with the sights, sounds, and smells of Zanzibar, offering an authentic shopping experience.

- Darajani Market: The most famous and bustling market in Stone Town, Darajani Market is a sensory overload of fresh produce, seafood, spices, and household goods. As you wander through its lively corridors, you'll encounter stalls piled high with tropical fruits, freshly caught fish, and the aromatic spices that Zanzibar is known for. It's the perfect place to experience the local culture and pick up ingredients to recreate the island's flavors at home.

- Forodhani Gardens Night Market: Located along the waterfront, this vibrant evening market transforms into a hub of street food vendors offering local delicacies like Zanzibari pizza, grilled seafood, and fresh sugar cane juice. Although it's more of a food market, it's an experience you shouldn't miss, and you'll also find vendors selling crafts and small souvenirs.

- Slave Market and Auction House: While primarily a historical site, the former Slave Market also has a small market nearby where you can buy crafts and locally made products. It's a somber place to visit but offers insight into Zanzibar's history while also supporting local artisans.

2. Souvenirs: Treasures to Bring Home

Stone Town is known for its diverse range of souvenirs, many of which are hand-crafted by local artisans using traditional methods. Here are some popular items to look out for:

- Spices: Known as the "Spice Island," Zanzibar's most iconic export is its spices. You'll find a variety of high-quality spices like cloves, cinnamon, cardamom, vanilla, and black pepper. These are often sold in neatly packaged sets that make for perfect gifts or personal cooking use. Spice tours outside of Stone Town also offer opportunities to buy spices directly from farms.

- Kanga and Kitenge Fabrics: These colorful and patterned fabrics are an essential part of Swahili culture. Kanga is a rectangular cotton fabric typically worn by women, often adorned with vibrant designs and Swahili proverbs. Kitenge, on the other hand, is a wax-printed fabric often used to make clothing or bags. Both fabrics are available at markets and shops, and many vendors offer custom tailoring services to turn them into unique garments.

- Hand-Carved Wooden Items: Zanzibar is famous for its intricate wood carvings, especially its iconic Zanzibar doors, which are often replicated in smaller souvenir versions. You can find beautifully crafted wooden boxes, picture frames, and other decorative items, often carved with Swahili and Arab-inspired designs. Makonde wood carvings, depicting figures and animals, are also popular and showcase the incredible skill of local artisans.

- Jewelry: Zanzibar is home to talented jewelry makers who craft unique pieces using materials like silver, coral, seashells, and gemstones. You'll find bracelets, necklaces, and earrings that incorporate elements of the sea and African culture. Tanzanite, a rare gemstone found only in Tanzania, is a coveted item, though it can be quite expensive.

- Handmade Soaps and Oils: Many small shops offer locally made beauty products, including organic soaps infused with clove, cinnamon, or lemongrass, as well as coconut oils and natural body scrubs. These items make excellent gifts and offer a way to bring the scents of Zanzibar back home.

3. Local Crafts: A Showcase of Artisan Skill

Zanzibar's artisan community produces an impressive array of handcrafted items, and supporting these local crafts is a great way to contribute to the island's economy while taking home a piece of its culture.

- Tinga Tinga Art: This vibrant painting style originated in Tanzania and has become popular in Zanzibar. Tinga Tinga art is characterized by bold colors and whimsical depictions of animals, nature, and everyday life. You'll find both original pieces and reproductions for sale in galleries and markets. Many artists in Stone Town have small studios where you can watch them work and purchase directly from them.

- Zanzibar Chests: These ornately carved chests were once used by wealthy merchants and are now sought-after as decorative furniture. Made from teak or mahogany, they are intricately decorated with brass or copper fittings and geometric patterns. While buying a full-sized chest may be challenging to transport, smaller versions and replicas are widely available.

- Traditional Baskets and Weaving: Local women in Zanzibar are skilled at weaving baskets, mats, and hats using natural fibers such as palm leaves and sisal. These items are not only beautiful but also practical, often used by locals for storing food or carrying goods. The designs are simple yet elegant, and they make for wonderful, authentic souvenirs.

- Handmade Leather Goods: Leather craftsmanship is another important part of Zanzibar's artisan scene. You'll find handmade sandals, belts, bags, and wallets, often crafted with intricate patterns or embellishments. Many of these items are made using traditional methods and local materials, ensuring a durable and unique product.

4. Where to Shop: Top Stores and Boutiques

Beyond the bustling markets, Stone Town is home to a number of boutiques and craft shops where you can find high-quality items in a more relaxed shopping environment.

- Memories of Zanzibar: A one-stop shop for tourists, Memories of Zanzibar offers a wide range of souvenirs, from spices and textiles to jewelry and crafts. The prices are fixed, making it ideal for visitors who prefer not to haggle.

- The Gallery Zanzibar: Located in the heart of Stone Town, this boutique specializes in contemporary Tanzanian art, including Tinga Tinga paintings, as well as locally crafted jewelry and accessories. It's a great place to pick up unique pieces from talented artists.

- Cultural Arts Centre Zanzibar: This is not only a shopping destination but also a social enterprise supporting local artisans. The center offers a range of handmade products, from woven baskets and bags to handcrafted jewelry and textiles. It's a great way to buy authentic goods while contributing to the local economy.

- Khamis Leather Craft: For handmade leather goods, Khamis Leather Craft is one of the best-known shops in Stone Town. You'll find beautifully made sandals, belts, and bags that showcase the skill of Zanzibar's leatherworkers.

Shopping in Stone Town is an immersive experience that goes beyond buying souvenirs. It's an opportunity to connect with local artisans, learn about Zanzibar's history, and take home a piece of the island's rich cultural heritage. From bustling markets to quiet boutiques, the variety of local crafts and products available makes Zanzibar a true shopping paradise.

3.6. Local Cuisine and Coffee Houses: Where to Eat in Stone Town

Local Cuisine

1. Lukmaan Restaurant: Located on New Mkunazini Road, Lukmaan is a popular spot for both locals and tourists. It offers a variety of traditional Zanzibar dishes, including biryani, pilau, and grilled seafood. The casual

atmosphere and affordable prices make it a great place to experience authentic local flavors.

2. Forodhani Gardens: This open-air food market is a must-visit in the evenings. Located by the waterfront, it features numerous stalls selling freshly grilled seafood, Zanzibar pizza, sugar cane juice, and other local delicacies. It's a lively spot where you can enjoy a meal while watching the sunset over the Indian Ocean.

3. Emerson Spice Tea House Restaurant: Situated in a beautifully restored historic building, this restaurant offers a unique dining experience with a rooftop setting. The menu features a fusion of Swahili and international cuisines, with dishes like coconut curry and seafood platters. Reservations are recommended due to its popularity.

4. Zanzibar Coffee House Café: Located in a historic building on Mkunazini Street, this café offers a range of Swahili dishes and freshly brewed coffee. The café is

known for its cozy atmosphere and delicious breakfast options, including chapati and mandazi.

5. The Silk Route: This restaurant on Shangani Street offers a blend of Indian and Zanzibari cuisines. The menu includes dishes like tandoori chicken, seafood curry, and vegetarian options. The elegant setting and attentive service make it a great choice for a special meal.

Coffee Houses

1. Puzzle Coffee Shop: Located near Tippu Tip's House, Puzzle Coffee Shop is known for its specialty coffee and homemade pastries. The café has a relaxed atmosphere, making it a perfect spot to unwind with a cup of coffee and a book.

2. Zanzibar Coffee House: This café is part of the Zanzibar Coffee House Hotel and offers a touch of magic and romance in an authentic Arabic house. It serves some of the best coffee in Stone Town, along with

a selection of cakes and pastries. The rooftop terrace provides stunning views of the town.

3. Stone Town Café: Situated in the heart of Stone Town, this café is a favorite among tourists. It offers a variety of coffee drinks, smoothies, and light meals. The friendly staff and cozy ambiance make it a great place to relax after exploring the town.

4. Lazuli Café: Known for its healthy and delicious meals, Lazuli Café offers fresh seafood, juices, and smoothies. The relaxed and inviting atmosphere makes it a perfect spot for a meal with friends.

5. Unique53 Café Zanzibar: Located opposite the Slave Market, Unique53 Café offers a range of coffee drinks and light snacks. The café is known for its friendly service and comfortable seating, making it a great place to take a break from sightseeing.

These dining spots provide a wonderful opportunity to experience the rich culinary traditions and vibrant coffee culture of Stone Town.

3.7. Guided Walking Tours: Hidden Gems and Cultural Insights

Exploring Stone Town through a guided walking tour is one of the best ways to uncover its hidden gems and gain deep cultural insights.

1. Zanzibar Stone Town Walking Tour
This popular tour takes you through the winding streets of Stone Town, highlighting its rich history and cultural heritage. You'll visit key landmarks such as the Old Fort, House of Wonders, and the Sultan's Palace. The tour also includes stops at local markets and shops, where you can experience the vibrant local life.

2. Stone Town Historical Walking Tour
This tour focuses on the historical aspects of Stone Town, providing detailed insights into its past. You'll

explore significant sites like the Anglican Cathedral, built on the site of the former slave market, and the Hamamni Persian Baths. The knowledgeable guides share stories about the town's diverse influences and historical events.

3. 3-Hour Private Stone Town Walking Tour

For a more personalized experience, consider a private walking tour. This tour allows you to explore Stone Town at your own pace, with a guide who can tailor the experience to your interests. You'll visit major attractions and discover lesser-known spots, gaining a deeper understanding of the town's unique character.

4. Spice Tour + Stone Town Tour

This combined tour offers a comprehensive experience, starting with a visit to a spice farm where you can learn about Zanzibar's famous spices. After the spice tour, you'll head to Stone Town to explore its historical sites and cultural landmarks. This tour provides a great balance of nature and history.

5. Full Day Holiday Package (Prison Island, Stone Town, Spice Farm)

This full-day tour covers multiple attractions, including a visit to Prison Island, known for its giant tortoises and historical significance. You'll then explore Stone Town and finish with a tour of a spice farm. This package is perfect for those who want to see as much as possible in one day.

Hidden Gems and Cultural Insights

1. Freddie Mercury House

Located in the heart of Stone Town, this house is the birthplace of the legendary Queen frontman, Freddie Mercury. The house has been converted into a small museum, showcasing memorabilia and photographs of his early life in Zanzibar.

2. Princess Salme Museum

This museum is dedicated to Princess Salme, a Zanzibari princess who fled to Germany and wrote an autobiography detailing her life. The museum offers a fascinating glimpse into her life and the history of Zanzibar's royal family.

3. Forodhani Gardens

In the evenings, Forodhani Gardens transforms into a bustling food market, offering a variety of local dishes and snacks. It's a great place to sample Zanzibari cuisine and enjoy the lively atmosphere.

4. Peace Memorial Museum

Also known as Beit el Amani, this museum houses a collection of artifacts and exhibits related to Zanzibar's history, culture, and natural history. It's a lesser-known attraction that provides valuable insights into the island's past.

5. Dhow Countries Music Academy

This music academy is dedicated to preserving and promoting the traditional music of the Swahili coast. Visitors can attend performances and workshops, gaining a deeper appreciation for the region's musical heritage.

These guided tours and hidden gems offer a comprehensive and enriching experience of Stone Town, allowing you to delve into its history, culture, and vibrant local life.

Chapter 4: Zanzibar's Top Beaches and Coastal Life

4.1. The Northern Paradise: Nungwi and Kendwa

Nungwi and Kendwa, located on the northern tip of Zanzibar, are renowned for their stunning beaches, vibrant nightlife, and crystal-clear waters. These neighboring villages offer a perfect blend of relaxation and adventure, making them must-visit destinations for any traveler to Zanzibar.

Nungwi
1. Beaches and Water Activities
Nungwi is famous for its pristine white-sand beaches and turquoise waters. Unlike other parts of Zanzibar, the tides here are less extreme, allowing for swimming and water activities throughout the day. Popular activities include snorkeling, diving, and dhow sailing trips.

2. Nungwi Beach

Nungwi Beach is one of the most beautiful beaches in Zanzibar, known for its soft sand and stunning sunsets. The beach is lined with resorts, bars, and restaurants, offering plenty of options for dining and entertainment.

3. Mnarani Marine Turtles Conservation Pond

This conservation project is dedicated to the protection of endangered sea turtles. Visitors can learn about the conservation efforts and even participate in feeding the turtles.

4. Nungwi Village Tour

A guided tour of Nungwi village provides insights into the local culture and way of life. You can visit traditional dhow-building sites, local markets, and meet the friendly residents.

5. Nightlife

Nungwi is known for its lively nightlife, with numerous beach bars and clubs offering music, dancing, and entertainment well into the night. It's a great place to experience the vibrant social scene of Zanzibar.

Kendwa

1. Kendwa Beach

Just south of Nungwi, Kendwa Beach is another stunning stretch of sand known for its calm waters and beautiful sunsets. The beach is perfect for swimming, sunbathing, and beach sports.

2. Full Moon Party

Kendwa is famous for its monthly Full Moon Party, held at Kendwa Rocks. This event attracts visitors from all over the island for a night of music, dancing, and celebration under the full moon.

3. Diving and Snorkeling

The waters around Kendwa are ideal for diving and snorkeling, with vibrant coral reefs and abundant marine life. Several dive centers offer courses and guided trips for all levels of experience.

4. Relaxed Atmosphere

Compared to Nungwi, Kendwa offers a more laid-back vibe. It's an excellent spot for those looking to relax and unwind in a serene environment. The beach is less crowded, making it perfect for a peaceful getaway.

5. Accommodation Options

Kendwa has a range of accommodation options, from luxury resorts to budget-friendly guesthouses. Many of these places offer beachfront views and easy access to the beach.

Nungwi and Kendwa are two of Zanzibar's most captivating destinations, each offering unique experiences. Whether you're looking for adventure, relaxation, or a mix of both, these northern paradises have something for everyone. Enjoy the stunning beaches, vibrant culture, and unforgettable sunsets that make Nungwi and Kendwa truly special.

4.2. Paje and Jambiani: Zanzibar's Kite Surfing and Water Sports Hub

Paje and Jambiani, located on the southeast coast of Zanzibar, are renowned for their excellent kitesurfing conditions and vibrant water sports scene. These neighboring villages offer a perfect blend of adventure and relaxation, making them ideal destinations for water sports enthusiasts.

Paje

1. Kitesurfing

Paje is considered one of the best kitesurfing spots in Zanzibar. The shallow lagoon, protected by an offshore reef, provides flat water conditions ideal for beginners and freestyle riders. The consistent side-onshore winds, especially during the Kusi season (June to September) and the Kaskazi season (December to March), make it a kitesurfer's paradise.

2. Kite Schools and Rentals

There are several kite schools in Paje, such as Kite Centre Zanzibar and Zanzibar Kite Paradise, offering lessons for all skill levels and equipment rentals. These schools provide professional instruction and modern gear, ensuring a safe and enjoyable learning experience.

3. Other Water Sports

In addition to kitesurfing, Paje offers a variety of other water sports, including stand-up paddleboarding (SUP), windsurfing, and snorkeling. The calm, clear waters are perfect for exploring the vibrant marine life and coral reefs.

4. Beach Vibe

Paje has a laid-back atmosphere with a lively beach scene. The beach is lined with bars, restaurants, and accommodations ranging from budget-friendly hostels to luxury resorts. The nightlife in Paje is vibrant, with beach parties and events happening regularly.

Jambiani

1. Kitesurfing

Jambiani offers similar kitesurfing conditions to Paje but with fewer crowds. The long sandbank and shallow lagoon provide a safe and calm environment for kitesurfing. The winds are reliable, making it a great spot for both beginners and experienced riders.

2. Kite Schools and Rentals

Jambiani has several kite schools, such as Sharazād Kite & Watersport Centre and Coconuts Kite Zanzibar, offering lessons and equipment rentals. These schools cater to all levels of kitesurfers and provide a friendly and supportive learning environment.

3. Other Water Sports

Apart from kitesurfing, Jambiani is also popular for diving, snorkeling, and SUP. The clear waters and rich marine life make it an excellent spot for underwater exploration.

4. Relaxed Atmosphere

Jambiani is known for its relaxed and tranquil vibe. The village is less developed than Paje, offering a more authentic and peaceful experience. It's a great place to unwind and enjoy the natural beauty of Zanzibar.

Paje and Jambiani are two of Zanzibar's top destinations for kitesurfing and water sports. Whether you're a beginner looking to learn or an experienced rider seeking new challenges, these villages offer the perfect conditions and facilities. Enjoy the stunning beaches, consistent winds, and vibrant local culture that make Paje and Jambiani truly special.

4.3. Exploring the Pristine Sands of Matemwe

Matemwe, located on the northeastern coast of Zanzibar, is a tranquil village known for its stunning beaches, vibrant marine life, and serene atmosphere.

Matemwe Beach

Matemwe Beach is one of the most beautiful and unspoiled beaches in Zanzibar. The long stretch of white sand, lined with palm trees, offers a peaceful retreat away from the busier tourist spots. The beach is perfect for sunbathing, leisurely walks, and enjoying breathtaking sunrises.

Marine Activities

1. Snorkeling and Diving

Matemwe is renowned for its proximity to the Mnemba Atoll, one of the best snorkeling and diving spots in Zanzibar. The clear waters and vibrant coral reefs are home to a diverse array of marine life, including tropical fish, sea turtles, and dolphins. Several local operators offer snorkeling and diving excursions to Mnemba Atoll.

2. Fishing

The village of Matemwe has a strong fishing tradition. Visitors can join local fishermen on traditional dhow boats for a fishing trip, experiencing the local way of life and possibly catching their own dinner.

3. Seaweed Farming

Matemwe's economy is largely based on seaweed farming. Visitors can learn about this important local industry and see the seaweed farms along the coast. It's a unique cultural experience that provides insight into the daily lives of the villagers.

Accommodation

Matemwe offers a range of accommodation options, from luxury resorts to charming guesthouses.

1. Matemwe Lodge

This luxury lodge offers stunning ocean views, spacious bungalows, and excellent amenities, including a spa and infinity pool. It's an ideal choice for those looking to indulge in comfort and tranquility.

2. Zanzibar Sunrise at Bandas

A mid-range option with beachfront bandas (bungalows), this resort provides a relaxed atmosphere and easy access to the beach. It's perfect for travelers seeking a balance of comfort and affordability.

3. Kasha Boutique Hotel

This boutique hotel offers private villas with plunge pools, set in lush gardens overlooking the ocean. It's a great choice for couples and honeymooners looking for a romantic getaway.

Dining

Matemwe has several excellent dining options, offering a mix of local and international cuisine:

1. Marlin Restaurant

Located near the beach, Marlin Restaurant serves fresh seafood and Swahili dishes. The relaxed setting and friendly service make it a popular choice among visitors.

2. Furaha Local Restaurant

This local eatery offers a variety of traditional Zanzibar dishes, including grilled fish, curries, and chapati. It's a great place to experience authentic local flavors.

3. Bin Jabir Restaurant

Known for its healthy and delicious meals, Bin Jabir Restaurant offers a range of African and seafood dishes. The casual atmosphere and beachfront location make it a perfect spot for a leisurely meal.

Matemwe is a hidden gem on Zanzibar's northeastern coast, offering pristine beaches, rich marine life, and a peaceful atmosphere. Whether you're looking to relax on the beach, explore the underwater world, or immerse yourself in local culture, Matemwe has something for everyone.

4.4. Kizimkazi: Dolphin Spotting and Fishing Villages

Kizimkazi, located on the southern tip of Zanzibar, is a charming fishing village renowned for its excellent dolphin spotting opportunities and rich cultural heritage.

Dolphin Spotting

Kizimkazi is famous for its dolphin tours, which attract visitors from around the world. The village is home to both bottlenose and humpback dolphins, which can often be seen swimming close to the shore. The best time for dolphin spotting is early in the morning when the waters are cooler, and the dolphins are more active.

1. Dolphin Tours

Several local operators offer dolphin tours, typically lasting 2-3 hours. These tours usually start from the Kizimkazi Fishing Village and involve a boat trip out to the dolphin habitats. While sightings are not guaranteed, the experience of being out on the water and potentially swimming with dolphins is unforgettable.

2. Snorkeling

In addition to dolphin spotting, many tours include snorkeling opportunities. The clear waters around Kizimkazi are perfect for snorkeling, allowing you to see a variety of marine life, including colorful fish, sea turtles, and coral reefs.

Fishing Villages

Kizimkazi is not just about dolphins; it's also a traditional fishing village with a rich cultural history. The village is divided into two parts: Kizimkazi Dimbani and Kizimkazi Mkunguni.

1. Local Life

Visiting Kizimkazi offers a glimpse into the daily lives of the local fishermen. You can see traditional dhow boats being built and repaired, and watch as fishermen bring in their daily catch. This provides a unique cultural experience and a chance to learn about the traditional fishing methods used in Zanzibar.

2. Historical Sites

Kizimkazi is home to the oldest mosque in East Africa, the Kizimkazi Mosque, which dates back to the 12th century. This mosque is a significant historical and cultural site, offering insights into the early spread of Islam in the region. Visitors can explore the mosque and learn about its history and architecture.

3. Community Interaction

Engaging with the local community is a highlight of visiting Kizimkazi. Many tours and activities are run by local residents, providing an opportunity to support the community and learn directly from those who call Kizimkazi home.

Kizimkazi offers a unique blend of natural beauty, wildlife encounters, and cultural experiences. Whether you're dolphin spotting, snorkeling, or exploring the fishing village, Kizimkazi provides a memorable and enriching experience.

4.5. Michamvi Peninsula: Quiet Retreats and Beach Getaways

The Michamvi Peninsula, located on the southeastern coast of Zanzibar, is a serene and picturesque destination known for its pristine beaches, tranquil atmosphere, and stunning sunsets.

Michamvi Beach

Michamvi Beach is divided into two main areas: Michamvi-Pingwe and Michamvi-Kae. Both offer long stretches of white sand, clear blue waters, and a sense of seclusion that is ideal for relaxation.

1. Michamvi-Pingwe

Michamvi-Pingwe is famous for its beautiful beaches and the iconic Rock Restaurant, which is perched on a coral outcrop and accessible by foot during low tide or by boat during high tide[1]. The area is perfect for sunbathing, swimming, and exploring the intertidal zones where you can find starfish, clams, and colorful tropical fish.

2. Michamvi-Kae

Michamvi-Kae, on the western side of the peninsula, is known for its breathtaking sunsets over Chwaka Bay. The calm waters and serene environment make it an excellent spot for kayaking, stand-up paddleboarding, and beach walks.

Accommodation

Michamvi offers a range of accommodation options, from luxury resorts to boutique hotels, all designed to provide a peaceful and comfortable stay.

1. Kichanga Lodge

This eco-friendly lodge offers charming bungalows set in lush gardens with stunning ocean views. It's a perfect choice for those looking to disconnect and enjoy nature.

2. Michamvi Sunset Bay Resort

Located on the western side of the peninsula, this resort offers spacious rooms, a beautiful pool, and direct access to the beach. It's ideal for watching the sunset and enjoying a quiet retreat.

3. Upendo Zanzibar

A luxury boutique hotel located near the Rock Restaurant, Upendo Zanzibar offers stylish villas with private pools and direct beach access. It's perfect for a romantic getaway or a luxurious escape.

4. Karafuu Beach Resort & Spa

This resort offers a variety of accommodation options, from garden rooms to beachfront villas. It features multiple restaurants, a spa, and a range of activities, making it a great choice for families and couples alike.

5. Ras Michamvi Beach Resort

Set on a cliff overlooking the Indian Ocean, this resort offers stunning views, comfortable rooms, and a peaceful atmosphere. It's a great spot for relaxation and enjoying the natural beauty of Michamvi.

Activities

1. Snorkeling and Diving

The nearby Blue Lagoon and the fringe reef offer excellent snorkeling and diving opportunities. The clear waters and vibrant marine life make it a must-do activity for underwater enthusiasts.

2. Kite Surfing

Michamvi is also a great spot for kite surfing, with consistent winds and beautiful scenery. Several local operators offer lessons and equipment rentals for all skill levels.

3. Beach Walks and Exploration

The long, unspoiled beaches of Michamvi are perfect for leisurely walks and exploration. The low tide reveals fascinating intertidal zones where you can discover marine life and enjoy the natural beauty of the area.

4. Relaxation and Wellness

Many resorts in Michamvi offer spa services, yoga classes, and wellness programs. It's an ideal destination for those looking to relax, rejuvenate, and enjoy a slower pace of life.

The Michamvi Peninsula is a hidden gem on Zanzibar's southeastern coast, offering a perfect blend of tranquility, natural beauty, and luxury. Whether you're looking to relax on the beach, explore the underwater world, or enjoy a romantic getaway, Michamvi has something for everyone.

4.6. Best Beachfront Restaurants and Bars

Zanzibar is home to some incredible beachfront restaurants and bars where you can enjoy delicious food, refreshing drinks, and stunning ocean views.

1. The Rock Restaurant

Located on a rock in the Indian Ocean near Michamvi Pingwe, The Rock Restaurant is one of Zanzibar's most iconic dining spots. Accessible by foot during low tide and by boat during high tide, it offers a unique dining experience with fresh seafood and breathtaking views.

2. Beach House Zanzibar

Situated in Stone Town, Beach House Zanzibar is a vibrant beachfront restaurant and bar known for its sunset views and lively atmosphere. The menu features a mix of traditional Zanzibari and international dishes, making it a great spot for both locals and tourists.

3. Mr. Kahawa

Located in Paje, Mr. Kahawa is a popular beachfront café and bar offering a relaxed vibe and stunning ocean views. It's a great place to enjoy a coffee, smoothie, or light meal while watching the kitesurfers in action.

4. Kendwa Rocks Beach Hotel

Kendwa Rocks Beach Hotel is famous for its Full Moon Party, but it also has a fantastic beachfront restaurant and bar. Enjoy a variety of dishes, from fresh seafood to international cuisine, while soaking in the beautiful beach scenery.

5. Coral Rocks Zanzibar

Situated in Jambiani, Coral Rocks Zanzibar offers a laid-back atmosphere with a beachfront bar and restaurant. The menu features a mix of local and international dishes, and the bar is a great place to enjoy a cocktail while watching the sunset.

These beachfront spots provide the perfect setting to relax, dine, and enjoy the natural beauty of Zanzibar. Whether you're looking for a romantic dinner, a casual lunch, or a lively night out, these restaurants and bars have something to offer.

Chapter 5: Outdoor Adventures and Activities.

5.1. Scuba Diving and Snorkeling: Top Spots and Marine Life

Scuba Diving Spots:

1. Mnemba Atoll: This spot is famous for its vibrant coral reefs and abundant marine life, including whale sharks, manta rays, and a resident pod of dolphins. It's suitable for all levels, with dive sites ranging from deep walls to coral gardens.

2. Nungwi Reefs: Known globally as a top scuba diving location, Nungwi Reefs offer diverse marine species and excellent visibility, making it ideal for both beginners and experienced divers.

3. Pemba Island: Pemba Island features underwater caverns and drift dives, with sightings of turtles,

dolphins, and a variety of reef fish. It's best for more experienced divers due to the challenging conditions.

4. Leven Bank: This spot is known for its strong currents and large pelagic species, including barracudas and trevallies. It's recommended for advanced divers.

Snorkeling Spots:

1. Nungwi Beach: With easy shore access, Nungwi Beach has a sandy drop-off and coral patches, perfect for spotting clownfish, lionfish, and sea stars. It's great for all snorkelers, including beginners.

2. Mnemba Island: The reef fringing the northern shore of Mnemba Island is bustling with marine life, making it Zanzibar's busiest snorkeling spot. It's suitable for all levels, with both shore and boat access.

3. Blue Lagoon: Offering both shore and boat snorkeling, Blue Lagoon has clear waters and a variety of reef fish, making it accessible for all snorkelers.

4. Jambiani Beach: Known for its shallow waters and rich marine biodiversity, Jambiani Beach is perfect for beginners and families, with colorful reef fish and sea urchins.

Marine Life:

Zanzibar's waters are teeming with life. You can expect to see reef fish like clownfish, butterflyfish, and surgeonfish. Larger species such as whale sharks, manta rays, and dolphins are often spotted, especially around Mnemba Atoll. The coral reefs are vibrant and diverse, home to over 500 marine species. Unique creatures like nudibranchs, ghost pipefish, and porcelain crabs add to the underwater spectacle.

5.2. Kite Surfing: Paje's Famous Winds and Lessons

Paje Beach is renowned for its ideal kite surfing conditions, making it one of the top destinations for this thrilling sport. Here's what you need to know about kite surfing in Paje:

Winds and Conditions:

- Wind Patterns: Paje benefits from consistent side-onshore winds. From mid-June to mid-October, the Kusi wind blows from the southeast, and from December to mid-March, the Kaskasi wind comes from the northeast.

- Water Conditions: The protective reef creates a lagoon with calm, shallow waters, perfect for both beginners and advanced kite surfers.

Kite Surfing Lessons:

- Kite Centre Zanzibar: This center offers lessons for all levels, from beginners to advanced riders. They provide professional instruction and top-notch equipment.

- Zanzibar Kite Paradise: Known for its experienced instructors and modern equipment, this school offers personalized lessons tailored to your skill level.

- Aquaholics Kite & Surf: Located right on Paje Beach, they offer lessons, coaching, and tailored boat trips, ensuring a comprehensive kite surfing experience.

5.3. Sailing and Deep-Sea Fishing in Zanzibar's Waters

Sailing:

Zanzibar offers a fantastic sailing experience with its clear blue waters and steady winds. You can choose from various sailing options, including traditional wooden dhows, luxurious catamarans, and yachts. Popular sailing activities include:

- Sunset Cruises: Enjoy a relaxing evening on the water, watching the sun set over the Indian Ocean.
- Snorkeling Trips: Combine sailing with snorkeling to explore the vibrant coral reefs and marine life.
- Private Charters: Tailor your sailing experience to your preferences, whether it's a romantic getaway or a family adventure.

Deep-Sea Fishing:

Zanzibar is a prime destination for deep-sea fishing, offering thrilling opportunities to catch big game fish.

- Fishing Charters: Numerous operators offer fishing charters, providing all necessary equipment and experienced guides. Some popular options include Zanzibar Angler's Paradise and Fishing Zanzibar Co Ltd.
- Target Species: The waters around Zanzibar are home to a variety of game fish, including marlin, sailfish, yellowfin tuna, wahoo, barracuda, and dorado.
- Best Spots: The Pemba Channel and the waters around Mnemba Island are renowned for their rich fishing grounds.
- Fishing Techniques: You can try different techniques such as trolling, jigging, and bottom fishing, depending on the species and conditions.

5.4. Safari Blue Tour: Island Hopping and Sandbank Adventures

The Safari Blue Tour in Zanzibar is one of the most popular and enchanting sea adventures you can experience on the island. This full-day excursion offers a variety of activities that showcase the natural beauty and rich marine life of Zanzibar.

Highlights of the Safari Blue Tour

1. Traditional Dhow Sailing: You'll sail on a traditional wooden dhow, a type of boat that has been used in the Indian Ocean for centuries. The journey itself is a unique experience, offering stunning views of the coastline and the open sea.

2. Snorkeling: The tour includes guided snorkeling sessions in some of the best spots around the island. You'll get to explore vibrant coral reefs and encounter a variety of tropical fish. Quality snorkeling equipment is provided, ensuring a safe and enjoyable experience.

3. Sandbank Stop: One of the highlights is a stop at a pristine sandbank where you can relax, swim, and soak up the sun. It's a perfect spot for taking photos and enjoying the serene environment.

4. Mangrove Lagoon: You'll also have the chance to swim in a natural mangrove lagoon. This unique ecosystem is home to a variety of marine life and offers a tranquil setting for a refreshing swim.

5. Seafood Buffet Lunch: A delicious seafood buffet is served on Kwale Island, featuring freshly caught fish, lobster, calamari, and other local delicacies. The meal is complemented by a tasting of tropical fruits, providing a true taste of Zanzibar.

6. Dhow Sailing Back: After a day of adventure, you'll sail back to Fumba village, enjoying the beautiful sunset over the Indian Ocean.

Additional Options

- Private Charter: For a more personalized experience, you can opt for a private dhow charter. This includes a dedicated crew, a customized itinerary, and a private lunch in a secluded spot.
- Bubble Boat: Another exclusive option is the Bubble Boat, which offers a private boat and table at the restaurant on Kwale Island, along with a selection of drinks and extra comfort.

The Safari Blue Tour is not just about the activities; it's also about the warm hospitality and the opportunity to learn about the local culture and environment. The tour operators are committed to sustainability, minimizing their environmental footprint, and supporting the local community.

5.5. Walking and Cycling Trails in Zanzibar

Zanzibar offers a variety of walking and cycling trails that allow you to explore its stunning landscapes, rich culture, and vibrant wildlife.

Walking Trails

1. Jozani Forest: This is one of the most popular walking trails in Zanzibar. The forest is home to the rare Red Colobus monkeys and offers a chance to explore lush vegetation and diverse wildlife. Guided tours are available to help you learn more about the flora and fauna.

2. Michamvi-Pingwe: This trail starts from Michamvi and takes you along the beach towards Pingwe. It's a relatively easy walk, perfect for observing sea birds and local fishermen at work.

3. Mangrove Walks: Near Michamvi, you can also explore the mangrove forests. These walks are best done with a guide who can explain the importance of mangroves to the local ecosystem.

4. Stone Town: A walking tour of Stone Town is a must. This UNESCO World Heritage site is rich in history and culture, with narrow streets, bustling markets, and historical buildings.

Cycling Trails

1. Stone Town to Jambiani: This route takes you from the historic Stone Town to the beautiful beaches of Jambiani. It's a long ride, covering about 110 km, but offers a mix of urban and rural scenery.

2. Nungwi and Northern Tip: This trail leads to the northern tip of the island, passing through the village of Nungwi. You'll see palm-lined beaches, local boatyards, and even some Portuguese ruins.

3. Matemwe and Northeast Region: This route takes you through peaceful beaches and green rice farms. It's a great way to see the agricultural side of Zanzibar and enjoy some quiet time by the sea.

4. Red Earth Village Route: This unique trail takes you through a village built on deep red soil. You'll get to meet local residents and learn about their customs and traditions.

5. Off-Road to Hidden Beach: For the more adventurous, this off-road trail leads to a secluded beach known only to locals. It's a challenging ride but offers stunning views and a sense of adventure.

5.6. Birdwatching and Exploring Zanzibar's Wildlife

Zanzibar is also a paradise for nature enthusiasts, offering a rich tapestry of wildlife and birdwatching opportunities.

Birdwatching in Zanzibar

1. Jozani Forest: This is one of the best spots for birdwatching in Zanzibar. The forest is home to over 40 species of birds, including the Zanzibar red bishop, Fischer's turaco, and the mangrove kingfisher. The diverse habitats, from mangroves to coastal forests, provide a haven for both resident and migratory birds.

2. Mnemba Island: Known for its marine life, Mnemba Island also attracts a variety of seabirds. It's a great spot to see species like the crab plover and various terns.

3. Pongwe Forest Reserve: Located on the northeastern coast of Unguja, this reserve is home to around 47 bird

species. It's a quieter spot, perfect for birdwatchers looking to escape the crowds.

4. Kidike Root Site: Situated in the central part of Pemba Island, this site is renowned for its bird diversity, hosting over 240 species.

Exploring Zanzibar's Wildlife

1. Jozani Chwaka Bay National Park: This park is the only national park in Zanzibar and is famous for the endangered Zanzibar red colobus monkey. The park also hosts other wildlife such as the Zanzibar servaline genet, bush babies, and various antelope species.

2. Cheetah's Rock: A unique conservation center where you can interact closely with rescued animals, including cheetahs, lions, and bush babies. It's a great place to learn about wildlife conservation efforts in Zanzibar.

3. Zanzibar Land Animal Park (ZALA): Located in Muungoni Village, this park is home to a variety of

animals, including tortoises, vervet monkeys, and bush crabs.

4. Marine Life: Zanzibar's waters are teeming with marine life. You can spot dolphins, sea turtles, and a myriad of fish species while snorkeling or diving around the island.

Chapter 6: Zanzibar's Nature and Wildlife

6.1. Jozani Forest: Exploring the Red Colobus Monkeys

Jozani Forest, located in the heart of Zanzibar's only national park, offers an exceptional experience for nature lovers and wildlife enthusiasts. The forest is most famous for being home to the endangered Zanzibar Red Colobus Monkeys, a species found nowhere else in the world. These monkeys are known for their striking red and black fur, white bellies, and expressive faces. Unlike other monkeys, they are not afraid of humans, making it possible to observe them up close as they leap from tree to tree or feed on leaves.

A visit to Jozani Forest is more than just an encounter with the Red Colobus Monkeys. The forest itself is a thriving ecosystem of tropical trees, mangroves, and swampy areas, providing habitat for a variety of wildlife, including Sykes' monkeys, bush babies, and the rare Zanzibar Leopard. The guided tours offer insight into the forest's unique biodiversity and the conservation efforts to protect it.

Walking through the forest's trails, you'll also hear the sounds of native birds and spot colorful butterflies. The mangrove boardwalk provides a serene setting to learn about this important habitat. Jozani Forest is not just a wildlife haven but also a crucial area for the island's environmental conservation efforts.

Visiting Jozani Forest is a year-round activity, but the best time to visit is during the dry season, from June to September, when the weather is pleasant, and the trails are easier to navigate. The forest is approximately a 30-minute drive from Stone Town, Zanzibar's capital, and can be reached by taxi, private car, or public minibuses known as dala dalas.

6.2. Mangroves and Wetlands: A Diverse Ecosystem

Zanzibar's mangroves and wetlands are vital ecosystems that support a wide range of wildlife and play a crucial role in the island's environmental stability. Mangroves, with their intricate root systems, are found along the coastal areas and serve as natural buffers against erosion and storms, protecting the island's shorelines. These unique trees thrive in saline water and are home to various species of fish, crabs, and birds, making them essential for both marine life and biodiversity.

Wetlands, often found inland, are equally important, acting as natural water filters and habitats for diverse species, including amphibians, reptiles, and migratory birds. In Zanzibar, these areas are vital for supporting local fishing communities as they serve as breeding grounds for many fish species. Wetlands also regulate water flow, preventing flooding during the rainy season.

Together, mangroves and wetlands contribute significantly to Zanzibar's ecological balance. They provide essential resources for local communities while supporting the island's rich wildlife, making them critical for conservation and environmental sustainability efforts. Exploring these ecosystems offers insight into the delicate balance of nature and the need for their continued protection.

6.3. Chumbe Island: Coral Reefs and Conservation Projects

Chumbe Island, located off the coast of Zanzibar, is a stunning marine sanctuary renowned for its thriving coral reefs and groundbreaking conservation projects. The island's Coral Reef Sanctuary is one of the most pristine in the region, boasting over 200 species of coral and more than 400 species of fish, making it a paradise for snorkelers and marine enthusiasts. The clear, shallow waters offer an excellent opportunity to witness the vibrant underwater life, including colorful fish, sea turtles, and other marine creatures.

Beyond its natural beauty, Chumbe Island is a model for eco-tourism and marine conservation. Since 1994, the island has been a privately managed nature reserve, with a strong focus on protecting its biodiversity. The conservation projects on the island include coral monitoring, sustainable fishing practices, and environmental education programs for local communities. The island's eco-lodge, which operates using solar power and rainwater harvesting, supports these conservation efforts while offering visitors a sustainable stay in harmony with nature.

Chumbe Island's commitment to marine preservation and its diverse coral reefs make it a must-visit destination for anyone interested in marine biology, conservation, or simply enjoying the natural beauty of Zanzibar's waters.

6.4. Marine Reserves and Protected Areas in Zanzibar

Zanzibar is home to several marine reserves and protected areas dedicated to preserving the rich biodiversity of its waters. These conservation zones play a critical role in maintaining the health of marine ecosystems, protecting endangered species, and supporting sustainable tourism.

1. Mnemba Atoll Marine Reserve: One of Zanzibar's most popular marine conservation areas, Mnemba Atoll is renowned for its vibrant coral reefs and abundant marine life. The atoll is a haven for snorkelers and divers, offering encounters with species like dolphins, turtles, and colorful reef fish. The reserve's clear waters and diverse underwater environment make it a prime spot for marine exploration while ensuring the protection of coral reefs and habitats.

2. Menai Bay Conservation Area: Covering the southwest coast of Zanzibar, Menai Bay is the largest

marine protected area in the region. It's a key site for dolphin conservation, as well as mangrove forests and seagrass beds. Menai Bay also promotes sustainable fishing practices to support local communities while safeguarding marine biodiversity.

3. Chumbe Island Coral Park: This privately managed marine park is a leader in eco-tourism and conservation. The coral reefs surrounding Chumbe Island are among the most pristine in Zanzibar, and conservation projects focus on coral monitoring, reef restoration, and environmental education for locals.

These reserves are vital in protecting Zanzibar's marine life, preserving ecosystems, and promoting sustainable tourism.

Chapter 7: Culture and Traditions in Zanzibar

7.1. The Influence of Swahili Culture on Zanzibar's Identity

Swahili culture has profoundly shaped Zanzibar's identity, creating a unique blend of African, Arab, Persian, and Indian influences that reflect its rich history as a major trading hub. The Swahili people, primarily coastal dwellers along East Africa, have developed a culture that fuses traditions from different civilizations, which can be seen in Zanzibar's language, architecture, cuisine, and social customs.

Language: Swahili, or Kiswahili, is the dominant language in Zanzibar and a crucial marker of its cultural identity. Rooted in Bantu origins with heavy Arabic influences, the language reflects the island's historical role in trade and cultural exchange. Arabic words, drawn from Zanzibar's history as part of the Omani Sultanate, intermingle with African dialects, showcasing the island's cosmopolitan nature.

Architecture: The distinctive Swahili architecture of Stone Town, Zanzibar's cultural capital, is another example of this cultural fusion. The famous carved wooden doors, coral stone houses, and winding streets reveal both Arab and Indian craftsmanship, while the layout reflects centuries of African settlement.

Cuisine: Zanzibar's cuisine, heavily influenced by Swahili culture, is a flavorful mix of spices, seafood, and tropical fruits. Dishes like biryani, pilau, and ugali combine African cooking methods with spices brought from Arabia and India, cementing the island's identity as the "Spice Island."

Overall, Swahili culture, with its open embrace of different influences, defines Zanzibar's rich, multifaceted identity today.

7.2. Traditional Arts and Crafts: Wood Carving, Tinga Tinga, and Fabrics

Zanzibar is renowned for its rich tradition of arts and crafts, which reflect the island's diverse cultural heritage.

Wood carving is a highly respected art form in Zanzibar, with a long history of intricate craftsmanship. Artisans create detailed carvings from local hardwoods, often depicting animals, human figures, and abstract designs. These carvings are not only decorative but also hold cultural and spiritual significance. The Makonde people, in particular, are famous for their intricate carvings, known as Makonde sculptures, which often feature complex, interwoven figures and themes.

Tinga Tinga is a distinctive painting style that originated in Tanzania in the 1960s, named after its founder, Edward Saidi Tingatinga. This art form is characterized by its bold colors, whimsical themes, and simple yet expressive designs. Tinga Tinga paintings often depict animals, folklore, and scenes of daily life, capturing the vibrant spirit of East African culture. The style has become popular worldwide, and many artists in Zanzibar continue to create these lively and colorful works.

Fabrics play a significant role in Zanzibar's cultural expression. The island is known for its beautiful textiles, including kanga, kitenge, and batik. These fabrics are often brightly colored and feature intricate patterns and designs.

- Kanga: A traditional fabric worn by women, kanga is a rectangular piece of cloth with a border and a central design, often accompanied by a proverb or message. It is used for clothing, head wraps, and baby slings.
- Kitenge: Similar to kanga but typically thicker and more durable, kitenge is used for making dresses, skirts, and other garments. It is also popular for its vibrant patterns and is often worn during special occasions.
- Batik: This fabric is created using a wax-resist dyeing technique, resulting in unique and intricate patterns.

Batik is used for clothing, wall hangings, and other decorative items.

Visiting Zanzibar's Craft Markets

To experience these traditional arts and crafts firsthand, visitors can explore Zanzibar's bustling markets and craft shops. Stone Town is a great place to start, with its narrow streets lined with shops selling wood carvings, Tinga Tinga paintings, and colorful fabrics. The Darajani Market and Forodhani Gardens are also popular spots to find local crafts and souvenirs.

7.3. Local Etiquette and Social Customs: Do's and Don'ts for Tourists

When visiting Zanzibar, it's important to respect the local customs and social norms to ensure a pleasant and respectful experience.

Do's

1. Dress Modestly:

- Zanzibar is predominantly Muslim, so it's respectful to dress modestly, especially in Stone Town and rural areas. Women should cover their shoulders and knees, and men should avoid wearing shorts in public places.

2. Greet Locals:

- Greetings are an important part of Zanzibari culture. A simple "Jambo" (Hello) or "Habari" (How are you?) goes a long way. Use your right hand for handshakes.

3. Respect Religious Practices:

- During the call to prayer, it's respectful to pause and avoid loud activities. If you visit a mosque, dress appropriately and remove your shoes before entering.

4. Ask for Permission:

- Always ask for permission before taking photos of people, especially in rural areas. Some locals may not be comfortable being photographed.

5. Support Local Businesses:

- Buy souvenirs and crafts from local artisans to support the community. Bargaining is common in markets, but do so respectfully.

Don'ts

1. Avoid Public Displays of Affection:

- Public displays of affection, such as kissing and hugging, are considered inappropriate. Keep such gestures private.

2. Don't Drink Alcohol in Public:

- While alcohol is available in tourist areas, drinking in public places is frowned upon. Stick to designated areas like bars and restaurants.

3. Don't Point with Your Finger:

- Pointing with your finger is considered rude. Instead, use your whole hand to gesture.

4. Avoid Discussing Sensitive Topics:

- Topics such as politics and religion can be sensitive. It's best to avoid these in casual conversations with locals.

5. Don't Litter:

- Keep Zanzibar clean by disposing of trash properly. Littering is not only disrespectful but also harmful to the environment.

By following these guidelines, you can show respect for the local culture and enjoy a more enriching experience in Zanzibar.

Chapter 8: Zanzibar's Food and Culinary Experiences

8.1. Traditional Dishes: Ugali, Pilau, and Zanzibar Pizza

Zanzibar's culinary scene is a delightful blend of African, Arab, Indian, and European influences.

Ugali is a staple food in Zanzibar and across East Africa. It is a simple yet versatile dish made from maize flour (cornmeal) and water, cooked to a dough-like consistency. Ugali is typically served as an accompaniment to various stews, meats, and vegetables.

- Preparation: The maize flour is gradually added to boiling water and stirred continuously until it thickens and forms a dense, dough-like consistency.
- Serving: Ugali is usually served in a large communal bowl, and pieces are broken off and used to scoop up

accompanying dishes like meat stews, greens, or soured milk.

Pilau is a fragrant rice dish that is a favorite in Zanzibar. It is influenced by Indian and Middle Eastern cuisines and is known for its rich blend of spices.

- Ingredients: Pilau is made with rice, meat (often chicken or beef), and a variety of spices such as cinnamon, cardamom, cloves, and cumin. Sometimes, vegetables and dried fruits like raisins are added for extra flavor.
- Preparation: The meat is first cooked with onions and spices, then rice is added along with water or broth. The mixture is simmered until the rice is fully cooked and infused with the aromatic spices.
- Serving: Pilau is often served during special occasions and celebrations, accompanied by a side of kachumbari (a fresh tomato and onion salad) or a spicy chutney.

Zanzibar Pizza is a unique street food that has become a popular culinary attraction. Despite its name, it is quite different from the traditional Italian pizza.

- Ingredients: The base is made from a thin dough, which is filled with a variety of ingredients such as minced meat, vegetables, eggs, and cheese. Sweet versions with bananas and chocolate are also popular.
- Preparation: The dough is rolled out thin, filled with the chosen ingredients, and then folded over to form a pocket. It is then fried on a hot griddle until crispy and golden brown.
- Serving: Zanzibar Pizza is typically enjoyed as a snack or light meal and is best experienced at the Forodhani Night Market in Stone Town, where vendors prepare it fresh in front of you.

These traditional dishes offer a taste of Zanzibar's rich culinary heritage and are a must-try for any visitor. Enjoying these foods is not just about the flavors but also about experiencing the island's vibrant culture and history.

8.2. Seafood Specialties: Fresh Fish, Octopus, and Lobster

Zanzibar, surrounded by the bountiful Indian Ocean, is a paradise for seafood lovers.

Fresh fish is a staple in Zanzibari cuisine, with a variety of species available, including red snapper, kingfish, and tuna. The fish is often marinated in a blend of local spices such as turmeric, ginger, and garlic, then grilled to perfection.

- Grilled Fish: This is a popular dish where the fish is marinated and grilled over an open flame, giving it a smoky flavor. It is typically served with rice, vegetables, or French fries, especially in beachside restaurants.
- Fish Curry: Another favorite, fish curry is made with fresh fish cooked in a rich, spicy sauce with coconut milk, tomatoes, and a mix of local spices. It's usually served with rice or chapati.

Octopus is a beloved ingredient in Zanzibar, known for its tender texture and ability to absorb flavors well.

- Octopus Curry: This dish features octopus cooked in a fragrant curry sauce made with coconut milk, tomatoes, onions, and a variety of spices. It's a flavorful and hearty meal often enjoyed with rice or ugali.
- Grilled Octopus: Marinated in a mixture of spices and lemon juice, the octopus is grilled until tender and slightly charred, offering a deliciously smoky taste. It's often served with a side of salad or grilled vegetables.

Lobster in Zanzibar is a true delicacy, often enjoyed fresh from the ocean.

- Grilled Lobster: This is a must-try dish where the lobster is grilled and served with a side of rice or grilled vegetables. It's typically accompanied by dipping sauces such as garlic butter, lemon juice, or chili sauce.
- Lobster Thermidor: A more luxurious option, lobster thermidor involves lobster meat cooked in a creamy sauce with cheese and mustard, then baked until golden

brown. It's a rich and indulgent dish often served at high-end restaurants.

Where to Enjoy These Delicacies

- Forodhani Night Market: Located in Stone Town, this bustling market is a great place to sample a variety of seafood dishes, including grilled fish and Zanzibar pizza.
- Beachside Restaurants: Many restaurants along the beaches of Nungwi, Kendwa, and Paje offer fresh seafood dishes with stunning ocean views.
- Local Fish Markets: Visiting markets like the Darajani Market in Stone Town allows you to see the fresh catch of the day and even purchase seafood to cook yourself.

8.3. Spice Tour Cuisine: Cooking Classes and Local Delicacies

Zanzibar is famously known as the "Spice Island," and its rich culinary heritage is deeply intertwined with the spices grown on the island. A spice tour combined with a cooking class offers visitors a unique opportunity to explore this heritage and learn to prepare traditional Zanzibar dishes.

Spice tours typically take place on spice farms located in the lush countryside of Zanzibar. These tours provide an immersive experience where visitors can see, smell, and taste a variety of spices such as cloves, nutmeg, cinnamon, and vanilla.

- What to Expect: During a spice tour, knowledgeable guides explain the history and uses of each spice, often sharing fascinating anecdotes and traditional remedies. Visitors can taste fresh spices and fruits directly from the plants.
- Popular Spice Farms: Some well-known spice farms include Kizimbani and Kidichi, where you can see a wide range of spices and tropical fruits being cultivated.

Cooking Classes

After exploring the spice farms, many tours include a hands-on cooking class where participants can learn to prepare authentic Zanzibari dishes using the spices they've just discovered.

- Typical Dishes: Common dishes taught in these classes include pilau (spiced rice), biryani, coconut curries, and seafood specialties. Participants also learn to make traditional accompaniments like chapati (flatbread) and kachumbari (fresh tomato and onion salad).

- Experience: The cooking classes are usually led by local chefs who guide participants through each step of the cooking process, from preparing ingredients to cooking and finally enjoying the meal together. This interactive experience not only teaches cooking techniques but also provides insights into Zanzibar culture and traditions.

Local Delicacies

Zanzibar's cuisine is a delightful fusion of African, Arab, Indian, and European influences.

- Zanzibar Mix: A popular street food, this is a hearty soup made with potatoes, chickpeas, and a variety of spices, often served with fritters and a tangy tamarind sauce.

- Urojo: Another beloved street food, Urojo is a thick, spicy soup made with a mix of ingredients like potatoes, eggs, and crispy bhajias (fried snacks).

- Coconut Bread: Known locally as mkate wa nazi, this sweet and fragrant bread is made with coconut milk and is often enjoyed with tea or coffee.

Tips for Visitors

- Book in Advance: Spice tours and cooking classes are popular activities, so it's a good idea to book in advance, especially during peak tourist seasons.

- Dress Comfortably: Wear comfortable clothing and shoes suitable for walking around the spice farms.

- Bring a Camera: The vibrant colors and beautiful scenery of the spice farms make for great photo opportunities.

- Be Open to Tasting: Don't be afraid to try new flavors and dishes. The spices and foods of Zanzibar offer a unique culinary adventure.

Participating in a spice tour and cooking class is a fantastic way to immerse yourself in the flavors and culture of Zanzibar. It's an experience that not only delights the taste buds but also provides lasting memories of your visit to this beautiful island.

8.4. Dining Out: Zanzibar's Best Restaurants, Cafés, and Street Food

Zanzibar offers a wide variety of dining experiences, from elegant restaurants to bustling street food markets. The island's culinary scene is deeply influenced by Swahili, Arab, Indian, and European cuisines, offering visitors a delightful fusion of flavors.

1. Best Restaurants

- The Rock Restaurant: Located on a small rock island off the coast of Michamvi, this iconic restaurant offers stunning views of the Indian Ocean. Specializing in seafood, The Rock serves dishes like grilled lobster, prawns, and octopus, complemented by a rich selection of local spices.

- Emerson on Hurumzi: A must-visit in Stone Town, Emerson on Hurumzi is set in a historic building with a rooftop dining experience. The restaurant serves a multi-course Swahili feast, featuring traditional dishes such as biryani and pilau with a gourmet twist, alongside fresh seafood.

- Forodhani Gardens: While technically more of an open-air food market, Forodhani offers one of the best evening dining experiences in Zanzibar. The stalls here serve everything from grilled seafood skewers to Zanzibar pizza.

- Lukmaan Restaurant: A local favorite, Lukmaan in Stone Town is known for its affordable, authentic Swahili cuisine. Visitors can enjoy dishes like ugali, samaki wa kupaka (fish in coconut sauce), and a range of flavorful curries.

- Upendo Beach: Situated in Michamvi, this beachside restaurant offers a relaxed atmosphere with panoramic views of the ocean. Upendo Beach focuses on organic, local ingredients, serving fresh salads, seafood, and wood-fired pizzas.

2. Cafés

- Puzzle Coffee Shop: A cozy café in the heart of Stone Town, Puzzle offers locally sourced Zanzibari coffee and a selection of pastries and light meals. It's a great spot to relax and enjoy the laid-back vibe of the city.

- Stone Town Café: Located on Kenyatta Road, this café offers a welcoming environment with delicious breakfast options, fresh fruit juices, and Swahili snacks. Visitors can enjoy traditional Zanzibar coffee alongside dishes like chapati and samosas.

- Café Foro: Tucked away in Forodhani Gardens, Café Foro serves local teas, coffees, and light bites. It's a perfect stop for a quick snack or drink after a walk through the historical streets of Stone Town.

3. Street Food

- Zanzibar Pizza: Found at Forodhani Night Market, Zanzibar pizza is a street food must-try. This unique flatbread is stuffed with fillings like minced meat, egg, cheese, and vegetables, or even sweet fillings like Nutella and banana for dessert.

- Samosas and Mishkaki: Throughout Stone Town's winding streets, vendors sell freshly fried samosas and mishkaki (skewered, grilled meat). These snacks are perfect for a quick and flavorful bite while exploring the town.

- Urojo Soup: Also known as Zanzibar mix, urojo is a thick, spicy soup made from a base of turmeric and tamarind. It's served with fried snacks like bhajias and potato fritters, offering a mix of tangy and spicy flavors.

- Kaimati and Vitumbua: For something sweet, try local desserts like kaimati (fried dough soaked in syrup) or vitumbua (coconut rice cakes). These treats are widely available from street vendors and make for a perfect afternoon snack.

From gourmet dining to local street food, Zanzibar's diverse culinary offerings reflect its multicultural heritage, giving visitors a true taste of the island's flavors.

Chapter 9: Practical Tips for a Stress-Free Visit

9.1. Safety and Health in Zanzibar: Clinics, Hospitals, and Insurance

Zanzibar, a beautiful archipelago off the coast of Tanzania, is a popular destination for tourists. However, it's important to be aware of the safety and health services available to ensure a smooth and enjoyable stay.

Clinics and Hospitals

Zanzibar has a mix of public and private healthcare facilities. While public hospitals and clinics provide basic medical services, they may not meet the standards found in more developed countries. For more serious conditions, private clinics such as Tasakhtaa Global Hospital and Mnazi Mmoja Hospital are recommended as they offer better facilities and services.

Health Precautions

Before traveling to Zanzibar, it's advisable to get vaccinations for diseases such as typhoid, tetanus, diphtheria, polio, meningitis, and hepatitis A. Although the risk of contracting these diseases is low, it's better to be safe. Additionally, if you're coming from a Yellow Fever endemic zone, you will need to show a vaccination certificate upon arrival.

Malaria is present in Zanzibar, though the risk is lower compared to mainland Tanzania. It's important to take precautions such as using insect repellent, sleeping under mosquito nets, and wearing long-sleeved clothing, especially during the rainy seasons.

Travel Insurance

As of recent regulations, travel insurance is mandatory for visitors to Zanzibar. This insurance typically covers hospitalization, doctor visits, and emergency medical services within Zanzibar. It's designed to provide comprehensive health coverage during your stay, ensuring that you can receive necessary medical care without financial strain.

Safety Tips

Zanzibar is generally safe for tourists, but it's always wise to take standard precautions. Be mindful of your belongings, avoid walking alone at night, and respect local customs and traditions. Staying informed about local safety guidelines and health advisories can help you have a worry-free experience.

By taking these precautions and being aware of the available healthcare services, you can enjoy the stunning beauty and rich culture of Zanzibar with peace of mind.

9.2. Getting Around: Taxis, Daladalas, and Car Rentals

Navigating Zanzibar offers a mix of local and tourist-friendly transport options, allowing you to explore the island with ease. Whether you're looking for comfort, affordability, or adventure, Zanzibar's taxis, daladalas, and car rentals offer diverse ways to get around.

1. Taxis

Taxis are one of the most convenient ways to travel in Zanzibar, especially for tourists. They are widely available in Stone Town, at airports, hotels, and major tourist attractions. However, taxis in Zanzibar do not operate on meters, so it's essential to negotiate the fare before starting your journey.

- Private Taxis: These are great for airport transfers, hotel pickups, or day trips around the island. A typical ride from Stone Town to the northern beaches (Nungwi) costs around $30–$50 USD, while a shorter trip within Stone Town may cost $5–$10 USD.

- Tour Taxis: Many hotels and tour operators offer taxis for day trips to popular destinations like Jozani Forest, Paje Beach, or Spice Farms. These services are convenient for tourists who prefer organized transportation and are willing to pay a bit more for reliability and comfort.

2. Daladalas

For the more adventurous traveler, daladalas are an affordable and authentic way to get around Zanzibar. These are shared minivans or trucks converted into public buses, providing a local experience as you travel with Zanzibari residents. *Daladalas* have fixed routes and stop at major towns and villages across the island.

- Cost and Experience: Daladalas are incredibly cheap, with most rides costing between $0.20 to $1 USD, depending on the distance. They operate on a hop-on-hop-off basis, so you can catch one at any of the main bus stops or flag them down on the road. While daladalas are economical, they are often overcrowded, and schedules can be unpredictable, making them best suited for those seeking an authentic local experience.

- Routes: Common routes include Stone Town to Nungwi, Paje, Jambiani, and other coastal villages. Be prepared for a slow journey, as daladalas stop frequently to pick up and drop off passengers.

3. Car Rentals

Renting a car gives you the freedom to explore Zanzibar at your own pace. Car rentals are widely available, and driving around the island is relatively straightforward. However, you'll need to obtain a temporary Zanzibar driver's permit, which rental companies can arrange for you.

- Cost: Rental prices vary depending on the type of vehicle, but expect to pay around $30–$50 USD per day for a standard car. For a 4x4, which is ideal for off-road adventures or visiting more remote areas, prices range from $60–$100 USD per day.

- Driving in Zanzibar: Zanzibar follows left-hand driving, and the roads range from well-paved highways to bumpy dirt roads, especially in rural areas. Renting a car allows you to visit remote beaches, explore inland attractions like Jozani Forest, and discover hidden gems at your own leisure. Parking is generally easy to find, although driving through Stone Town can be tricky due to narrow streets.

- Motorbike Rentals: For those looking for a smaller and more flexible option, motorbikes and scooters are also available for rent. These are ideal for solo travelers or couples and cost around $10–$20 USD per day. Be sure to wear a helmet and drive cautiously, as local traffic can be unpredictable.

4. Bicycle Rentals

For eco-conscious travelers, renting a bicycle is an affordable and enjoyable way to explore Zanzibar, especially in coastal areas or small towns.

- Cost: Bicycles are available for rent at many hotels and guesthouses, with rates typically around $5–$10 USD per day.

- Ideal for: Cycling is a perfect option for exploring beach areas like Jambiani, Paje, or Nungwi, where the terrain is flat and distances between attractions are manageable. It's also a great way to take in the island's scenery at a leisurely pace. In Stone Town, you can cycle through the narrow streets, although caution is needed due to busy traffic in certain areas.

5. Walking

Walking is an excellent way to explore Zanzibar's towns and cities, especially Stone Town, where many attractions are located within walking distance of each other. The town's narrow, winding streets are best navigated on foot, allowing you to experience its rich history and vibrant atmosphere up close.

- Stone Town: As a UNESCO World Heritage site, Stone Town is perfect for walking tours. You can explore its historic sites, including the Old Fort, House of Wonders, and Darajani Market, while discovering hidden alleyways filled with local shops and cafés.

- Beaches: Many of Zanzibar's beaches, such as Nungwi, Jambiani, and Paje, are also great for walking, with long stretches of sand ideal for leisurely strolls.

Taxis provide comfort and convenience, daladalas offer a local, budget-friendly experience, renting a car gives you the freedom to explore the island independently, Bicycle rentals are great for eco-conscious travelers seeking adventure and Walking lets you fully immerse yourself in Zanzibar's culture and beauty. Each option has its advantages, depending on your travel preferences and itinerary.

9.3. Internet, SIM Cards, and Staying Connected

Staying connected in Zanzibar is essential for both tourists and digital nomads.

Internet Access

Internet in Zanzibar can be a bit inconsistent, but there are several options to stay connected:

- Hotels and Cafes: Many hotels, guesthouses, and cafes offer free Wi-Fi. However, the speed and reliability can vary greatly.

- Coworking Spaces: For those needing a more stable connection, coworking spaces in Stone Town provide reliable internet access.

- Mobile Data: Using mobile data is often the most reliable way to stay connected. This requires a local SIM card or an eSIM.

SIM Cards

Purchasing a local SIM card is straightforward and can save you from high roaming charges. Here are the main providers:

- Vodacom: Known for the best overall coverage and reliable 4G speeds.

- Airtel: Offers good coverage and competitive prices.

- Tigo: Another reliable option with decent coverage.

- Zantel: Recommended for its strong coverage in Zanzibar.

You can buy SIM cards at the airport, but prices are higher. It's better to purchase them from official stores in Stone Town or other major areas. Remember to bring your passport for registration.

eSIMs

For those with compatible devices, eSIMs are a convenient option. Providers like Airalo, Manet, and Holafly offer eSIMs that can be activated instantly, providing data without the need for a physical SIM card.

Tips for Staying Connected

- Top-Up: Use apps like MyVodacom to easily top up your data.

- Coverage: Stay near urban areas or signal towers for the best connection.

- Backup: Consider having a backup SIM or eSIM in case of network issues.

By choosing the right options for your needs, you can ensure a smooth and connected experience in Zanzibar.

9.4. Money Matters: ATMs, Credit Cards, and Local Banks

When traveling to Zanzibar, understanding how to manage your money is essential for a smooth trip. Everything you need to know about accessing funds, using credit cards, and navigating local banks.

1. ATMs

ATMs are the most convenient way to access cash while in Zanzibar, though they are not as widespread as in other tourist destinations. Most ATMs are located in Stone Town, at the airport, and in a few larger towns like Nungwi and Paje.

- Availability: In Stone Town, you'll find ATMs from major banks like Barclays, CRDB, NBC, and Equity Bank. ATMs are less common in rural or remote areas, so it's a good idea to withdraw cash before heading out of major towns.

- Currency Dispensed: ATMs in Zanzibar dispense Tanzanian Shillings (TZS), the local currency. Some ATMs may offer an option to withdraw in US dollars, but it's not guaranteed. It's advisable to carry both currencies, as some hotels and businesses accept USD, especially in tourist areas.

- Fees: ATM fees vary depending on your home bank and the ATM provider. Local banks typically charge a small fee, but your home bank may add international withdrawal fees, so check with them before traveling.

- Withdrawal Limits: The maximum withdrawal limit is typically around 400,000 Tanzanian shillings (approximately $160 USD) per transaction.

- Tips: Always withdraw more cash than you think you'll need, as ATMs can occasionally run out of money, especially on weekends or public holidays. It's also wise to carry small bills, as breaking larger denominations can sometimes be challenging.

2. Credit Cards

Credit cards are accepted at many mid-range to high-end hotels, restaurants, and tour operators in Zanzibar, but they are less commonly used for smaller purchases or in more remote areas.

- Where You Can Use Them: In tourist hubs like Stone Town, Nungwi, and Paje, you can use credit cards at most larger hotels, restaurants, and stores. However, smaller guesthouses, local restaurants, and markets generally operate on a cash-only basis.

- Fees and Surcharges: While credit cards are accepted in many places, businesses may apply a surcharge (often

3%–5%) to cover transaction fees. It's worth asking about this before making a purchase or booking.

- Card Types: Visa and MasterCard are the most widely accepted cards. American Express and other card networks may not be as widely used, so it's best to carry a backup Visa or MasterCard.

3. Local Banks

Zanzibar's banking system is linked with the mainland, and several national banks operate on the island. If you need to exchange currency, withdraw money, or conduct other banking activities, you'll find branches in Stone Town and other larger towns.

- Main Banks: The most prominent banks in Zanzibar include CRDB Bank, NBC Bank, Barclays, and NMB Bank. Most banks offer basic services like currency exchange, account management, and international transfers.

- Currency Exchange: While ATMs are convenient, banks and official exchange bureaus in Stone Town provide the best rates for exchanging foreign currency.

Avoid changing money at hotels or airports, where rates are often less favorable.

- Bank Hours: Banks are usually open Monday through Friday from 8:30 AM to 4:00 PM. Some banks also operate on Saturday mornings, but most are closed on Sundays and public holidays.

4. Currency and Tipping

The local currency in Zanzibar is the Tanzanian Shilling (TZS), but US dollars are also widely accepted, particularly in tourist areas. For larger expenses like hotel bills or tours, USD is often preferred. However, for smaller transactions, like local markets, restaurants, and taxis, having Tanzanian Shillings on hand is essential.

- Tipping: Tipping is appreciated but not mandatory in Zanzibar. In restaurants, a tip of 5%–10% is customary if service is not included. For taxis, rounding up to the nearest amount is polite, and for tour guides or hotel staff, small tips in either TZS or USD are appreciated.

5. Using Cash

Cash is king in Zanzibar, especially for small purchases, street food, or local markets. While USD is accepted in many places, having local currency for everyday expenses is recommended, especially if you're visiting rural areas or smaller shops.

Summary:

- ATMs are available but mainly in major towns. Always carry enough cash, especially when traveling to remote areas.
- Credit cards are accepted in high-end establishments, but expect to pay a surcharge.
- Local banks provide currency exchange services and are located in larger towns.
- Carry Tanzanian Shillings for small purchases, and consider tipping in local currency or USD.

Managing money in Zanzibar is straightforward if you plan ahead. Ensure you have both cash and cards to cover all types of transactions, and take advantage of ATMs and local banks in major towns.

Chapter 10: Zanzibar's Laws, Customs, and Visitor Etiquette

10.1. Important Legal Information: Drugs, Alcohol, and Public Behavior

When visiting Zanzibar, it's essential to familiarize yourself with local laws and customs, as they differ significantly from other parts of the world. Here's what you need to know about the legal status of drugs, alcohol, and expectations for public behavior during your stay.

1. Drugs
The possession, use, or distribution of drugs in Zanzibar is strictly illegal and heavily enforced. Tanzanian law

imposes severe penalties for drug-related offenses, including long prison sentences and hefty fines.

- Zero Tolerance: Zanzibar has a strict zero-tolerance policy toward narcotics, including cannabis, which may be legal or decriminalized in some other countries. Even small amounts can lead to severe consequences.
- Police Checks: Random police checks may occur, especially in areas frequented by tourists. If caught with illegal substances, you could face arrest, fines, and imprisonment.
- Prescription Drugs: If you are traveling with prescription medication, ensure you have a doctor's note or prescription, especially for controlled substances, to avoid complications.

2. Alcohol

Zanzibar is predominantly Muslim, and while alcohol is available, its consumption is regulated, and tourists should be respectful of local customs.

- Where to Drink: Alcohol is widely available in tourist areas, hotels, bars, and restaurants, particularly in Stone Town, Nungwi, and Kendwa. However, it is not sold in local shops or consumed in public areas in predominantly Muslim communities.

- Drinking in Public: Drinking alcohol in public places, outside designated venues, or on the streets is frowned upon and can lead to fines or trouble with local authorities.

- During Ramadan: During the Islamic holy month of Ramadan, alcohol may be harder to find, and many establishments may limit or cease its sale out of respect for the local Muslim population. It's important to be particularly mindful of cultural sensitivities during this time.

3. Public Behavior

Zanzibar is a conservative island with deeply rooted Islamic traditions, so it's important to dress modestly and behave respectfully, particularly in non-tourist areas.

- Dress Code: Modesty in dress is highly valued, especially in Stone Town and rural villages. Women should cover their shoulders and knees, while men should avoid going shirtless in public places. On the beach and in resorts, swimwear is acceptable, but it's advisable to cover up when leaving the beach area.

- Public Displays of Affection: Public displays of affection, such as kissing or hugging, are considered inappropriate in Zanzibar, especially outside tourist areas. Couples should avoid overly affectionate behavior in public to respect the local culture.

- Same-Sex Relationships: Homosexuality is illegal in Zanzibar, and LGBTQ+ travelers should be aware of the legal and cultural environment. Discretion is advised in public to avoid potential legal issues or social discomfort.

- Photography: Be mindful when taking photos, especially of local people, mosques, or religious gatherings. Always ask for permission before photographing individuals, as some locals may find it intrusive.

4. Respect for Religion

Zanzibar is an island where Islam plays a central role in daily life. Visitors should respect religious practices, such as prayer times and customs related to Ramadan.

- Mosques: Non-Muslims are generally not allowed to enter mosques unless they are part of a guided tour that provides appropriate context and respect for the space. Always remove shoes before entering, and dress modestly.
- Prayer Times: Be aware of the five daily prayers when loudspeakers may broadcast the call to prayer, and locals may briefly stop activities for worship.

5. Legal Penalties

Violating Zanzibar's laws on drugs, alcohol, or public behavior can result in arrest, fines, or imprisonment. It's crucial to respect local customs and obey the law to avoid any legal issues during your stay.

Understanding and respecting Zanzibar's laws and customs will ensure a smooth and enjoyable visit while fostering positive relations with the local community.

10.2. Environmental Responsibility: Protecting Zanzibar's Ecosystem

Zanzibar's stunning natural beauty and rich biodiversity make it a unique destination, but it's crucial to protect its delicate ecosystem. Some ways to be environmentally responsible while enjoying your time on the island:

Marine Conservation
- Coral Reefs: Zanzibar's coral reefs are home to diverse marine life. Avoid touching or stepping on corals, and use reef-safe sunscreen to prevent harmful chemicals from damaging the reefs.
- Marine Parks: Visit marine parks like Mnemba Atoll and Chumbe Island Coral Park, which focus on conservation and sustainable tourism. These parks often have guidelines to minimize human impact on marine life.

Waste Management

- Reduce Plastic Use: Bring a reusable water bottle and shopping bag to reduce plastic waste. Many hotels and restaurants are also moving towards eliminating single-use plastics.

- Proper Disposal: Dispose of waste properly and participate in beach clean-ups if possible. Keeping beaches clean helps protect marine animals from ingesting or getting entangled in plastic waste.

Wildlife Protection

- Respect Wildlife: Observe animals from a distance and avoid feeding or disturbing them. This helps maintain their natural behaviors and habitats.

- Support Ethical Tours: Choose tour operators that prioritize animal welfare and follow ethical guidelines for wildlife interactions.

Sustainable Practices

- Eco-Friendly Accommodations: Stay at eco-friendly lodges and hotels that implement sustainable practices such as solar power, water conservation, and waste recycling.

- Local Products: Support local artisans and businesses that use sustainable materials and practices. This not only helps the environment but also supports the local economy.

Energy and Water Conservation

- Conserve Resources: Be mindful of your water and energy use. Simple actions like taking shorter showers and turning off lights when not in use can make a big difference.

- Renewable Energy: Some accommodations use renewable energy sources like solar power. Opting for these places can reduce your carbon footprint.

Environmental Education

- Learn and Share: Educate yourself about Zanzibar's environment and share your knowledge with others. Many local organizations offer educational tours and programs that highlight conservation efforts.

By taking these steps, you can help protect Zanzibar's unique ecosystem and ensure that its natural beauty is preserved for future generations.

10.4. Responsible Tourism: Giving Back to the Local Community

When visiting Zanzibar, it's important to embrace the principles of responsible tourism, which not only enhances your travel experience but also helps protect the environment and supports the local community.

1. Support Local Businesses

One of the best ways to give back to the community is by supporting locally-owned businesses. This helps keep money circulating within the community and fosters economic growth for Zanzibaris.

- Stay Local: Choose to stay at locally-owned guesthouses, eco-lodges, and small hotels instead of large, international chains. These accommodations often have a lower environmental impact and directly benefit local families.

- Shop at Local Markets: Visit Zanzibar's markets and craft stalls, where artisans sell handmade products such as wood carvings, Tinga Tinga paintings, and traditional fabrics. Purchasing from these vendors supports local artists and preserves traditional crafts.

- Eat Local: Opt for locally-owned restaurants and cafés that serve Zanzibari cuisine. This not only supports the local economy but also allows you to experience authentic flavors using fresh, locally-sourced ingredients.

2. Engage in Cultural Exchange

Engage with the local community in respectful and meaningful ways to create a mutually beneficial cultural exchange.

- Respect Traditions: Learn about Swahili culture and traditions, and be mindful of local customs regarding dress, behavior, and religious practices. This fosters respect and understanding between tourists and locals.

- Participate in Local Tours: Join locally-operated tours, such as spice tours, walking tours, or village visits, to gain deeper insight into Zanzibari life. These tours are often run by local guides who can provide authentic perspectives and insights into the island's culture and history.

3. Volunteer and Contribute to Social Projects

Some visitors choose to contribute their time and skills to local social initiatives that address critical needs, such as education, health, and environmental conservation.

- Environmental Projects: Consider participating in beach cleanups, coral reef conservation projects, or mangrove planting efforts to protect Zanzibar's delicate ecosystems. Some eco-lodges and NGOs organize these activities, allowing tourists to contribute in a hands-on way.
- Community Support: Volunteer at schools, health clinics, or community development programs if you have the time. Some organizations on the island welcome

short-term volunteers to assist with education or health initiatives.

- Donations: If you're not able to volunteer, consider donating to local NGOs or community projects that support education, healthcare, or environmental protection in Zanzibar.

4. Be Mindful of Environmental Impact

Tourism can have a significant impact on the environment, so it's important to travel sustainably and minimize your footprint.

- Conserve Resources: Limit your water and energy usage, especially in accommodations that rely on local resources. Zanzibar faces water shortages, so being mindful of your consumption can make a difference.
- Reduce Waste: Avoid single-use plastics by carrying reusable water bottles and bags. Some hotels and lodges are committed to reducing plastic waste and provide refillable water stations.
- Respect Wildlife: When visiting marine reserves, forests, or conservation areas, be respectful of the

wildlife and ecosystems. Avoid touching coral reefs, feeding animals, or disrupting their natural habitats.

5. Fair Wages and Ethical Practices

Ensure that the businesses you support treat their employees fairly and provide fair wages. Responsible hotels, tour operators, and restaurants often highlight their commitment to fair employment practices.

By traveling responsibly, you can help ensure that Zanzibar remains a vibrant, welcoming destination for future visitors while empowering the local community and protecting its environment.

Chapter 11. A 5 Days Zanzibar Itinerary

Zanzibar Island, a jewel in the Indian Ocean off the coast of Tanzania, boasts stunning white sand beaches and mesmerizing turquoise waters. However, it offers much more than just picturesque coastlines. Historically significant as a key location in the East African slave trade, Zanzibar's rich cultural tapestry is woven from British, Portuguese, and Omani influences, making it a true melting pot.

The island's history is palpable, serving as a crossroads of African, European, Middle Eastern, and Indian cultures. This diverse heritage is most evident in the island's cuisine and architecture, particularly in the historic Stone Town.

Known as the Spice Islands, Zanzibar is home to numerous spice farms that welcome visitors for tours.

Here, you can learn about the cultivation of various spices and even participate in cooking classes.

In essence, Zanzibar Island offers far more than just its beautiful beaches. This 5-day itinerary is crafted to provide a perfect blend of adventure and cultural immersion, showcasing the best the island has to offer.

Day 1: Arrival and Stone Town Exploration
Morning: Your adventure begins as you land at Abeid Amani Karume International Airport. Upon arrival, you'll be greeted by a friendly driver who will transfer you to your hotel in Stone Town. This historic part of Zanzibar City is a UNESCO World Heritage Site, known for its rich cultural heritage and unique architecture.

Late Morning: After settling into your hotel and freshening up, your guide will meet you for a walking tour of Stone Town. This tour is a journey through time, showcasing the diverse influences that have shaped Zanzibar. As you wander through the narrow, winding streets, you'll notice the blend of African, Arab, Indian, and European architectural styles. Admire the intricately carved wooden doors, grand old buildings, and bustling markets.

Key Sites to Visit:
- House of Wonders (Beit-al-Ajaib): This iconic building, once a sultan's palace, now houses a museum showcasing Zanzibar's history and culture.
- Old Fort (Ngome Kongwe): Built by the Omani Arabs in the 17th century, this fort has served various purposes over the centuries and now hosts cultural events and a market.
- Anglican Cathedral and Slave Market: This poignant site marks the location of the former slave market. The cathedral, built by the British in the late 19th century, stands as a memorial to the victims of the slave trade. Inside, you'll find a moving altar built over the site of the old whipping post.

Afternoon: Enjoy a traditional Swahili lunch at a local restaurant. Savor dishes like pilau rice, biryani, and fresh seafood, all seasoned with the island's famous spices.

After lunch, continue your exploration with a visit to the Darajani Market. This bustling market is the heart of Stone Town, where locals shop for fresh produce, spices, and everyday goods. It's a sensory overload of sights, sounds, and smells, offering a true taste of local life.

Evening: As the sun sets, head to Forodhani Gardens, a popular spot for both locals and tourists. The evening food market here is a must-visit. Sample a variety of local delicacies such as Zanzibar pizza, grilled seafood, and sugarcane juice. The lively atmosphere, with the ocean as a backdrop, makes for a perfect end to your first day.

Day 2: Spice Tour and Dhow Cruise
Morning: Start your day with a visit to one of Zanzibar's renowned spice farms. Zanzibar is often referred to as the "Spice Island" due to its history as a major producer of spices. On this tour, you'll learn about the cultivation and uses of various spices like cloves, nutmeg, cinnamon, and vanilla. The tour is a feast for the senses, allowing you to see, smell, and taste the spices that have

shaped the island's history. You'll also get to sample some exotic fruits and enjoy a traditional Swahili lunch prepared with fresh spices from the farm.

Afternoon: After the spice tour, return to Stone Town and prepare for a romantic dhow cruise. These traditional wooden sailing vessels have been used for centuries along the East African coast. Your afternoon cruise will take you along the coast, offering stunning views of Stone Town from the water. Relax on the deck as the dhow glides through the turquoise waters, and enjoy the cool sea breeze.

Evening: As the sun begins to set, the dhow cruise becomes even more magical. The sky transforms into a canvas of vibrant colors, providing a perfect backdrop for a memorable evening. Some cruises offer refreshments and snacks, allowing you to enjoy a light meal as you sail. The gentle rocking of the boat and the sound of the waves create a serene and romantic atmosphere.

Return to Hotel: After the cruise, return to your hotel in Stone Town. You might want to take a leisurely evening stroll through the town or relax at a rooftop bar, enjoying the night views and reflecting on the day's experiences.

These first two days offer a perfect blend of cultural immersion, historical exploration, and relaxation, setting the stage for an unforgettable Zanzibar vacation.

Day 3: Transfer to Beach Resort and Relaxation
Morning: After breakfast, check out from your hotel in Stone Town and prepare for a scenic drive to one of Zanzibar's idyllic beach resorts. Depending on your chosen resort, you might head to the northern beaches of Nungwi or Kendwa, or the eastern shores of Paje or Jambiani. The journey offers a glimpse of Zanzibar's lush landscapes and rural life.

Late Morning: Arrive at your beach resort, where you'll be welcomed with a refreshing drink and a warm smile. Check into your room and take some time to settle in. The resort's serene environment, with its swaying palm trees and pristine beaches, sets the perfect tone for relaxation.

Afternoon: Spend the afternoon exploring the resort's amenities. Many resorts offer a range of activities, from water sports like snorkeling, diving, and kayaking to land-based activities such as beach volleyball and yoga. If you prefer a more laid-back approach, lounge by the pool or on the beach, soaking up the sun and enjoying the gentle ocean breeze.

Lunch: Enjoy a leisurely lunch at the resort's restaurant, where you can savor fresh seafood and other local delicacies. Many resorts pride themselves on their culinary offerings, often featuring ingredients sourced from local farms and fishermen.

Evening: As the day winds down, treat yourself to a spa session. Many beach resorts in Zanzibar offer luxurious spa treatments that incorporate local spices and essential oils, providing a truly rejuvenating experience. Afterward, head to the beach to watch the sunset.

Zanzibar's sunsets are legendary, painting the sky with hues of orange, pink, and purple.

Dinner: End your day with a romantic dinner at the resort. Whether you choose a beachfront setting or a cozy indoor restaurant, the ambiance and cuisine are sure to make it a memorable evening. Some resorts also offer themed nights with live music or traditional dance performances, adding a touch of local culture to your dining experience.

Day 4: Free Day at the Beach
Morning: Wake up to the sound of the waves and enjoy a hearty breakfast at the resort. Today is all about relaxation and enjoying the beach at your own pace. Start your day with a walk along the shoreline, feeling the soft sand beneath your feet and the warm sun on your skin.

Mid-Morning: If you're feeling adventurous, take advantage of the water sports offered by the resort. Snorkeling and diving are particularly popular, as

Zanzibar's waters are home to vibrant coral reefs and diverse marine life. Alternatively, you can rent a kayak or paddleboard and explore the coastline from the water.

Lunch: Return to the resort for lunch, or if you're feeling adventurous, head to a nearby beach restaurant. Many local eateries offer delicious Swahili dishes and fresh seafood, providing an authentic taste of Zanzibar.

Afternoon: Continue your day of leisure with more beach activities or simply relax with a good book under the shade of a palm tree. If you're interested in exploring further, consider an optional excursion. Popular choices include a visit to Jozani Forest to see the red colobus monkeys or a trip to Prison Island to meet the giant tortoises and learn about the island's history.

Evening: As the sun sets, take a moment to reflect on your day while enjoying a cocktail or fresh coconut water. Zanzibar's beaches are known for their stunning sunsets, and this is the perfect time to capture some beautiful photos.

Dinner: For dinner, you might choose to dine at the resort or venture out to a local restaurant. Many beach areas have a variety of dining options, from casual beach bars to fine dining establishments. Enjoy your meal while listening to the sound of the waves and the gentle rustle of palm leaves.

Day 5: Beach Day and Departure

Morning: Start your final day in Zanzibar with a leisurely breakfast at your beach resort. Savor the fresh tropical fruits, pastries, and perhaps some local dishes like mandazi (Swahili doughnuts) or chapati. Take in the serene morning views of the ocean as you plan your last few hours on this beautiful island.

Mid-Morning: Spend your morning soaking up the sun on the beach. Whether you're staying in Nungwi, Kendwa, Paje, or Jambiani, the beaches are perfect for relaxation. Take a long walk along the shoreline, collecting seashells and enjoying the gentle waves. If you're feeling more active, you might want to go for a final swim or try out some water sports like paddleboarding or windsurfing.

Late Morning: If you haven't yet explored the underwater world, consider a snorkeling trip. Many resorts offer guided snorkeling tours to nearby reefs where you can see colorful fish, corals, and perhaps even sea turtles. It's a wonderful way to experience the marine biodiversity of Zanzibar one last time.

Lunch: Enjoy a relaxed lunch at a beachfront restaurant. Opt for fresh seafood, such as grilled fish or prawns, paired with local sides like coconut rice or plantains. The laid-back atmosphere and stunning views make for a perfect dining experience.

Afternoon: After lunch, take some time to explore the local area. Visit a nearby village to get a glimpse of daily life in Zanzibar. You can interact with locals, learn about their customs, and perhaps purchase some handmade crafts as souvenirs. This is a great way to support the local community and take home a piece of Zanzibar's culture.

Late Afternoon: Return to your resort and prepare for departure. Take a final stroll on the beach, capturing some last-minute photos of the breathtaking scenery. Pack your bags and check out of your room, ensuring you have all your belongings.

Evening: Your driver will transfer you to Abeid Amani Karume International Airport for your departure. Reflect on the incredible experiences you've had over the past five days – from exploring the historic streets of Stone Town to relaxing on pristine beaches and immersing yourself in the local culture.

As you board your flight, you'll carry with you the memories of Zanzibar's warm hospitality, vibrant culture, and stunning natural beauty. This trip has offered a perfect blend of adventure, relaxation, and cultural immersion, leaving you with unforgettable moments and a deep appreciation for this unique island paradise.

Conclusion

As you've journeyed through this guide, it's clear that Zanzibar is much more than just a tropical paradise. It's a destination where centuries of history, culture, and natural beauty converge to create an experience that is truly unique. Whether you've wandered the labyrinthine streets of Stone Town, soaked in the sun on Nungwi Beach, or explored the vibrant ecosystems of Jozani Forest and the surrounding marine reserves, Zanzibar offers something for every traveler.

From the island's rich Swahili culture and the legacy of the spice trade to its stunning coral reefs and conservation efforts, Zanzibar's charm lies in its diversity. This guide has aimed to highlight the very best the island has to offer—its unforgettable festivals, mouthwatering cuisine, vibrant art, and welcoming people.

But Zanzibar is more than a destination to visit—it's a place to connect, reflect, and appreciate the world around you. By traveling responsibly and supporting local businesses, you can contribute to preserving the island's heritage and natural beauty for generations to come.

Whether you're seeking adventure, relaxation, or cultural immersion, Zanzibar has it all. As your journey here comes to a close, we hope that this guide has prepared you well and sparked a deeper curiosity for all that this remarkable island has to offer. Safe travels, and may your memories of Zanzibar last a lifetime.

Printed in Great Britain
by Amazon